THE FRAMEWORK OF LANGUAGE

the framework of language
ROMAN JAKOBSON

michigan studies in the humanities

© 1980 by Roman Jakobson

Michigan Studies in the Humanities
Horace H. Rackham School of Graduate Studies

Library of Congress Cataloging in Publication Data

Jakobson, Roman, 1896–
    The framework of language.

    (Michigan studies in the humanities; no. 1)
    Includes bibliography.
    1. Linguistics—Collected works.   I. Title.
II. Series.
P27.J338   410   80-13842
ISBN 0-936534-00-1

CONTENTS

Preface   vi

Introduction (by Ladislav Matejka)   vii

A Glance at the Development of Semiotics   1

A Few Remarks on Peirce,
    Pathfinder in the Science of Language   31

Glosses on the Medieval Insight
    into the Science of Language   39

The Twentieth Century in European and
    American Linguistics: Movements and Continuity   61

Metalanguage as a Linguistic Problem   81

On Aphasic Disorders from a Linguistic Angle   93

On the Linguistic Approach to the Problem
    of Consciousness and the Unconscious   113

PREFACE

With this volume, *Michigan Studies in the Humanities* inaugurates a series of books designed to promote cooperation among the various branches of the humanities by presenting perspectives on traditional problems of interpretation and evaluation. Though written by scholars firmly grounded in their special fields, these works will attempt to reach a wider audience by acknowledging problems confronted by the many branches of humanistic endeavor. At a time when scholars seem to speak to a narrower and narrower audience, it becomes essential that the common framework of humanistic investigation must be reasserted. We believe that the specialization and fragmentation of our field can be transcended and, without the trivializing effects of popularization, a sense of shared purpose can invigorate separate investigations and create a context for a unified understanding of human creativity and imagination.

Michigan Studies in the Humanities is directed by an editorial board representing a broad spectrum of scholars in the humanities and social sciences; initial funding for the publications is provided by the Horace H. Rackham School of Graduate Studies at the University of Michigan. We hope, however, that the series will become selfsupporting in the near future.

INTRODUCTION

The ever expanding bibliography of Roman Jakobson's contributions to the humanities recently prompted an editor of one of the numerous *Festschrifts* in Jakobson's honor to dub him a "polyhistor,"[1] implying thereby that polyhistors did not altogether die out with the Goethes, von Humboldts and other late representatives of the Renaissance ideal of Universal Man. In Jakobson's case, however, selection of the *signans* 'polyhistor' is adequate only if its broad semantic load, i.e. its *signatum,* is constrained by the fact that Jakobson has always remained faithful to his adopted coat of arms, *Linguista sum: linguistici nihil a me alienum puto.*

Indeed, in all Jakobson's forays into other fields, the linguistic view has prevailed to such an extent that he has sometimes been accused of promoting a linguistic imperialism. At any rate, linguistics clearly dominates his shifting network of relations, whether he discusses the molecular endowment of every *homo sapiens,* teleology in cybernetics, homologies of the genetic code, aphasic impairments, Hölderlin's madness, or three hypostases of the human essence in the likeness of the Trinity.

While insisting on dialogue with other fields and combatting the parochial tendencies of certain linguistic schools, Jakobson has always warned against the danger of surrendering the autonomy of linguistics and dissolving it in other fields, whether they be sociology, psychology, anthropology, neurology, logic or algebra. Since his early scholarly career, he has encouraged an interdisciplinary teamwork which would presuppose that each discipline must understand the language of other disciplines and, in turn, be understood by them. It was in this sense

1. C. H. van Schooneveld, "By Way of Introduction: Roman Jakobson's Tenets and Their Potential," *Roman Jakobson: Echoes of his Scholarship,* ed. by D. Armstrong and C. H. van Schooneveld (Lisse, 1978).

that he understood the term "structuralism," which he coined but abandoned when it turned into a fad causing a rapid swelling of the *signatum* and a truly pathological case of assymetric dualism of a verbal sign. And it is in the same sense that he uses the term "semiotic(s)."

For Jakobson semiotics is a framework for an interdisciplinary teamwork of specialists and certainly not an eclectic academic fashion which would not hesitate to use the concept of sign for hazy metaphors about exciting vistas to be opened by a new, all-embracing and all-encompassing unified science. He approaches the general study of signs as a linguist concerned not only with the similarities but also with the profound differences among various sign systems. In his view, the basic, the primary and the most important semiotic system is verbal language: "language," he emphatically asserts, "really is the foundation of culture; in relation to language, other systems of symbols are concomitant or derivative."[2]

The primacy of the verbal language and particularly the pervasive role of articulated sound is newly restated as a *summa summarum* in *The Sound Shape of Language* (1979), where Roman Jakobson, together with his co-author Linda Waugh, highlights the connection between the articulated sound of verbal communication and the phenomena of thought, emphatically rejecting all attempts to assume "wordless or even signless, asemiotic thinking."[3] And it is in the name of a qualitative hierarchy of various sign systems that Jakobson voices serious misgivings about the attempt of 'zoosemiotics' to downgrade the fundamental distinction between the verbal communication of man and the sign communication of bees, birds, apes and other species. In his view, "the transition from 'zoosemiotics' to human language is a huge qualitative leap, in contradiction to the outdated behaviourist creed that the language of animals differs from men's language in degree but not in kind."[4] Verbal language for Jakobson is 'species-specified,' and, as such, separated from all the various animal signs by a set of essential properties such as the imaginative and creative power of language, its ability to handle abstractions and fictions, and to deal with things and events remote in space and/or time. In this connection, Jakobson recalls the notion of double articulation' which, as a theory, originated in the Middle Ages, if not earlier, but was reformulated in

2. Roman Jakobson, "Results of a Joint Conference of Anthropologists and Linguists," *Selected Writings*, 2 (The Hague, 1971), p. 556.
3. Roman Jakobson and Linda Waugh, *The Sound Shape of Language*, (Bloomington, 1979).
4. Roman Jakobson, *Main Trends in the Science of Language* (New York, 1974), p. 45.

1930 by the Russian linguist D. Bubrix and more recently by the French structuralist André Martinet and others in their attempts to explain the privileged human ability of articulation as an operation of two subsequent steps: the articulation of sound matter *(articulatio prima)* and of words into sentences *(articulatio secunda).*

The results of numerous efforts to train individual anthropoids to use visual substitutes for human language strike Jakobson as "magnificent proofs of a deep chasm between human linguistic operations and the semiotic primitivism of apes."[5] He regards the differences as far more illuminating than the similarities and strongly advises that human language be kept apart from animal communication and that we avoid imposing anthropomorphic concepts on the general study of signs. This is one of the main themes of Jakobson's concise study "A Glance at the Development of Semiotics."[6] Jakobson insists here that the semiotic research which touches upon the question of language should avoid the imprudent application of the special characteristics of verbal language to other semiotic systems. And at the same time, he warns against attempts to exclude from semiotics "the study of systems of signs which have little resemblance to language and to follow up this ostracizing activity to the point of revealing a presumably 'non-semiotic' layer in language itself."

Although Jakobson in his writing has frequently given credit to Ferdinand de Saussure for his cursory remarks about the general science of signs, it is Charles Sanders Peirce who, in Jakobson's view, made the most substantial and lasting contribution to modern semiotics by his effort to illuminate diverse principles in the classification of signs and to challenge the simplified emphasis on arbitrariness in the concept of sign. Jakobson's paper, "A Few Remarks on Peirce," included in the present volume, was originally delivered as a lecture at Johns Hopkins University in Baltimore where Peirce spent five years of his life as a teacher, a rather exceptional period in his struggle for recognition by the American academic community. In Jakobson's view, Peirce's most felicitous contribution to general linguistics and semiotics is his definition of meaning as 'the translation of a sign into another systems of sign.' "How many fruitless discussions about mentalism and antimentalism would be avoided," Jakobson avers, "if one approached the notion of meaning in terms of translation, which no mentalists and no

5. *Ibid.*
6. It was originally delivered in French as the introductory speech to the First Congress of the International Association of Semiotics (IASS) in 1974. In its English version it appears for the first time in the present volume.

behaviorists could reject." This proclamation, however, should not be interpreted as Jakobson's impartiality in the struggle between mentalists and anti-mentalists. Anti-mentalism has for years been a target of his most vehement attacks. Recently he restated his position in an address to the Symposium on the European Background of American Linguistics, also included in the present volume. Here, blaming the impact of radical behaviorism on Leonard Bloomfield, Jakobson reminds us that "any 'mentalistic view' was proscribed by Bloomfield as a 'prescientific approach to human things' or even a 'primeval drug of animism' with its 'teleologic and animistic verbiage': will, wish, desire, volition, emotion, sensation, perception, mind, idea, totality, consciousness, subconsciousness, belief, and the other 'elusive spiritistic-teleologic words on our tribal speech'."

One of the concepts which the anti-mentalists, whether radical or moderate, have found hard to accept is, of course, that of metalanguage. Yet, metalanguage plays a fundamental role in Jakobson's 'Organon' of verbal communication, first outlined in his Presidential Address to the Annual Meeting of the Linguistic Society of America in 1956, and republished in our volume. Here Jakobson asserts that "metalingual operations with words or syntactic constructions permit us to overcome Leonard Bloomfield's forebodings in his endeavors to incorporate meaning into the science of language.

In Jakobson's struggle with anti-mentalism, it is, however, the acquisition of language and its decay which became his two paramount themes. His more recent contribution to this area is republished here from the *Scandinavian Journal of Logopedics and Phoniatrics* under the title "On Aphasic Disorders from a Linguistic Angle." In our volume, it is followed by his paper "On the Linguistic Approach to the Problem of Consciousness and the Unconscious" which is the English translation of his Russian paper for the *International Conference on the Unconscious* in October, 1979, in Tbilisi, URRS. The conference, we may point out, was basically initiated by the Georgian school of psychology, which has been struggling for years with the powerful anti-mentalistic forces dominating Soviet scholarship. Using this opportunity, Jakobson here again recalls his favored predecessors and fellow fighters for a broad interdisciplinary framework of scholarship: Baudouin de Courtenay, Mikołaj Kruszewski, Ferdinand de Saussure, Franz Boas and particularly Edward Sapir, who has been for Jakobson the most inspiring figures of modern American linguistics and anthropology.

Ladislav Matejka

THE FRAMEWORK OF LANGUAGE

A Glance at the Development of Semiotics

I

Emile Benveniste in his "A Glance at the Development of Linguistics" (*Coup d'oeil sur le développement de la linguistique*), [1963]), the beautiful study whose heading I borrow for this presentation, brings to our attention that "linguistics has a double object: it is the science of language and the science of languages . . . It is on languages that the linguist works, and linguistics is first of all a theory of languages. But . . . the infinitely diverse problems of languages have the following in common: at a certain degree of generality, they always put language into question." We are dealing with language as a universal invariant with respect to varied local languages which are variable in time and space. In the same order of things, semiotics is called to study the diverse systems of signs and to bring out the problems which result from a methodical comparison of these varied systems, that is to say, the general problem of the *SIGN*: sign as a generic notion with respect to the particular classes of signs.

The question of the sign and of signs was approached several times by the thinkers of Antiquity, of the Middle Ages and of the Renaissance. Around the end of the seventeenth century, John Locke's famous essay, in its final chapter on the tripartite division of the sciences, promoted this complex problem to the level of the last of the "three great provinces of the intellectual world" and proposed to call it "σημειωτική or the 'Doctrine of signs,' the most usual whereof being words," given that

to communicate our thoughts for our own use, signs of

our ideas are also necessary. Those which men have found most convenient, and therefore generally make use of, are articulate sounds (Book IV, Chapter XXI, Section IV).

It is to words, conceived of as "the great instruments of cognition," to their use and to their relation to ideas that Locke devotes the third book of his *Essay Concerning Humane Understanding* (1694).

II

From the beginning of his scientific activities, Jean Henri Lambert took account of the *Essay* and, while working on the *Neues Organon* (1764), which holds a pertinent spot in the development of phenomenological thought, he saw himself profoundly influenced by Locke's ideas, despite his taking a critical stance toward the sensualist doctrine of the English philosopher (*cf.* Eisenring, 1942: 7, 12, 48*ff.*, 82). Each of the two volumes of the *Neues Organon* is divided into two parts and, among the four parts of this whole treatise, the third—*Semiotik oder Lehre von Bezeichnung der Gedanken und Dinge,* followed by the *Phänomenologie*—inaugurates the second volume (pp. 3-214) of the work and owes to Locke's thesis the term *semiotic* as well as the theme of research, "the investigation of the necessity of symbolic cognition in general and of language in particular," (paragraph 6) given that this symbolic cognition "is to us an indispensible adjunct to thought" (paragraph 12).

In the preface to his work, Lambert warns us that he is working on language in nine chapters of the *Semiotik* (2-10) but allows only one chapter to other types of signs, "because language is not only necessary in itself and extraordinarily diffuse, but occurs with all other types of signs." The author wishes to devote himself to language, "in order to get to know its structure more closely" (paragraph 70) and to approach "general linguistics, *Grammatica universalis*, which is still to be sought." He reminds us

> that in our language the arbitrary, the natural and the necessary are blended. The primer of general linguistics should then mainly discuss the natural and the necessary, and the arbitrary, as far as is possible, sometimes on its own, sometimes in tight link with the natural and the necessary.

According to Lambert, the difference between these three elements which one finds in signs reveals a tight relationship with the decisive fact "that the first causes of language are in themselves already in human nature," and therefore this problem demands a meticulous examination (paragraph 13). The problem of algebra and of other systems of science's artificial languages with respect to natural languages (*wirkliche Sprachen*) is treated by Lambert (paragraph 55*ff*) as a sort of double translation (*gedoppelte Übersetzung*).

The book studies the difference in the use of natural and arbitrary signs (paragraphs 47 and 48); the natural signs of affects (*natürliche Zeichen von Affekten*) are those that first attract attention (paragraph 19). Lambert takes into account the significant role played by gestures, for example, "in order to enlighten the concept, which is dark in the soul [mind], . . . or at least to give an indication of it to ourselves and to others," and he foresees the semiotic scope of *simulacra* (which reappear after a century in Peirce's list under the labels of *icons* or *likenesses* [I.588]). Lambert raises the questions of signs whose internal structure is founded upon similarity relationships (*Ähnlichkeiten*) and, in interpreting signs of a metaphorical order, he evokes the effects of synesthesia (paragraph 18). Despite the summary character of his remarks on non-verbal communication, neither music, nor choreography, nor the blazon, nor the emblem,

nor ceremonies escapes the researcher's eye. The transformations of the signs (*Verwandlungen*) and the rules for
their combination (*Verbindungskunst der Zeichen*) are
placed on the agenda for further study.

III

It is because of Locke's and Lambert's creative
initiative that the idea and the name of semiotics reappear at the beginning of the nineteenth century. In his
early career, the young Joseph Marie Hoene-Wroński,
familiar with Locke's work, sketched, among other
speculative essays, a *Philosophie du language* which was
not published until 1879. The author, who is linked by
his disciple Jerzy Braun (1969) to Husserl's phenomenology and who is presented as "the greatest of
Polish thinkers," examines "the faculty of signation
(*facultas signatrix*)." The nature of signs (see p. 38)
must be studied first of all with respect to the categories of existence, that is to say, to the MODALITY
(proper/improper signs) and to the QUALITY (determined/
undetermined signs), and secondly with respect to the
categories of production, that is to say, to the QUANTITY
(simple/composite signs), to the RELATION (natural/
artificial signs) and the UNION (mediate/immediate
signs). Following Hoene-Wroński's program, it is the
"perfection of signs" ("perfection of language" in
Locke's terms, "*Vollkommenheit der Zeichen*" according to Lambert) which forms "the object of SÉMÉIO-
TIQUE" (p. 41). One should note that this theory
reduces the field of "signation" to acts of cognition,
"This signation is possible, whether for sensory form or
for sensory or intelligible content, of the objects of our

knowledge," while "the signation of acts of will and feeling" seems to be "impossible" (p. 38 *ff.*).

IV

The Prague philosopher, Bernard Bolzano, in his major work *The Theory of Science* [*Wissenschaftslehre*] (1837), mainly in the last two of the four volumes, reserves much space for semiotics. The author frequently cites Locke's *Essay* and the *Neues Organon,* and discovers in Lambert's writings "on semiotics . . . many very estimable remarks," though these are of little use "for the development of the most general rules of scientific discourse," one of the aims Balzano sets (paragraph 698).

The same chapter of *The Theory of Science* bears two titles, one of which—*Semiotik*—appears in the table of contents (vol. IV, p. xvi), the other of which—*Zeichenlehre*—heads the beginning of the text (p. 500); paragraph 637, which follows, identifies both designations—the theory of signs or semiotics (*Zeichenlehre oder Semiotik*). If, in this chapter and in several other parts of the work, the author's attention is held above all by the testing of the relative perfection of signs (*Vollkommenheit oder Zweckmässigkeit*) and particularly of signs serving logical thought, then it is in the beginning of the third volume that Bolzano tries to introduce the reader to the fundamental notions of the theory of signs throughout paragraph 285 (pp. 67-84) which overflows with ideas and is titled "the designation of our representations" (*Bezeichnung unserer Vorstellungen*).

This paragraph begins with a bilateral definition of the sign, "An object . . . through whose conception we wish to know in a renewed fashion another conception connected therewith in a thinking being, is known to us as a *sign*." A whole chain of geminate concepts follows, some of which are very new, while others referring back to their anterior sources, are newly specified and enlarged. Thus Bolzano's semiotic thoughts bring to the surface the difference between the meaning (*Bedeutung*) of a sign as such and the significance (*Sinn*) that this sign acquires in the context of the present circumstance, then the difference between the sign (1) produced by the addresser (*Urheber*) and (2) perceived by the addressee who, himself, oscillates between understanding and misunderstanding (*Verstehen und Missverstehen*). The author makes a distinction between the thought and expressed interpretation of the sign (*gedachte und sprachliche Auslegung*), between universal and particular signs, between natural and accidental signs (*natürlich und zufällig*), arbitrary and spontaneous (*willkürlich und unwillkürlich*), auditory and visual (*hörbar und sichtbar*), simple (*einzeln*) and composite (*zusammengesetzt,* which means "a whole whose parts are themselves signs"), between unisemic and polysemic, proper and figurative, metonymical and metaphorical, mediate and immediate signs; to this classification he adds lucid footnotes on the important distinction to be made between signs (*Zeichen*) and indices (*Kennzeichen*) which are devoid of an addresser, and finally on another pressing theme, the question of the relationship between interpersonal (*an Andere*) and internal (*Sprechen mit sich selbst*) communication.

V

The young Edmund Husserl's study, "*Zur Logik der Zeichen (Semiotik)*," written in 1890, but not published until 1970, is an attempt to organize the sign categories and to answer the question of knowing in which sense language, that is, our most important system of signs, "furthers and, on the other hand, once again inhibits thinking." Criticism of signs and their improvement are conceived of as an urgent task which confronts *logic*:

> A deeper insight into the nature of signs and of arts will rather enable [logic] to devise additionally such symbolic procedural methods upon which the human mind has not yet come, that is, to lay down the rules for their invention.

The 1890 manuscript contains a reference to the "*Semiotik*" chapter of *The Theory of Science* which is said to be *wichtig* (p. 530): in aiming at two targets in this essay, one structural and the other regulative, Husserl does in fact follow the example of Bolzano whom he will later call one of the greatest logicians of all time. In the semiotic ideas of the "*Logical Investigations*" one can find "decisive instigations from Bolzano" as the phenomenologist acknowledges; and the second volume of the *Investigations*, with its important treatise on general semiotics set up as a system, exerted a profound influence on the beginnings of structural linguistics. As Elmar Holenstein indicates, Husserl made several notes in the margins of paragraph 285 in his own copy of Bolzano's *The Theory of Science III* and he underlined the term *Semiotik* and its definition in Locke's *Essay* in its German translation *Über den menschlichen Verstand* (Leipzig, 1897).

VI

For Charles Sanders Peirce (1839-1914), the nature of signs remained a favorite subject of study since 1863 (*cf.* V.488 and VIII.376) and especially from the time of his magnificent profession of faith—"On a New List of Categories"—which was published in 1867 by the American Academy of Arts and Sciences (*cf.* I.545-559) thereupon followed two ingenious contributions to the *Journal of Speculative Philo-sophy* in 1868 (*cf.* V.213-317), and finally, materials collected in 1909-10 for his unfinished volume *Essays on Meaning* (*cf.* II.230-32; VIII.300; Lieb, 1953: 40).

It is notable that, throughout the thinker's whole life, the conception which underlies his continual efforts to establish a science of signs gained in depth and in breadth, and simul-taneously remained firm and unified. As for the "semio-tic," "semeiotic," or "semeotic," it only surfaces in Peirce's manuscripts at the turn of the century; it is at this time that the theory "of the essential nature and fundamental varieties of possible semiosis" captures the attention of this great researcher (I.444; v. 488). His insertion of the Greek σημειωτική as well as the concise definition "doctrine of signs" (II.277)—puts us on the track of Locke whose celebrated *Essay* was often referred to and cited by the doctrine's partisan. In spite of the marvelous profusion of original and salutary finds in Peirce's semiotics, the latter nonetheless remains tightly linked to his precursors—Lambert, "the greatest formal logician of those days" (II.346), whose *Neues Organon* is cited (IV.353), and Bolzano whom he knows by his "valuable contribution to the lucidity of human concepts" and by his "work on logic in four volumes" (IV.651).

Still Peirce declared rightly: "I am, as far as I know, a pioneer, or rather a backwoodsman, in the work of clearing and opening up what I call *semiotic*, . . . and I find the field too vast, the labor too great, for a first-comer" (V.488). It is he who is "the most inventive and the most universal of American thinkers" (*cf.* Jakobson, 1965:346), who knew how to draw up conclusive arguments and to clear the ground in order to erect at his own risk the framework of the scinece which two centuries of European philosophical thought had anticipated and foreseen.

Peirce's semiotic edifice encloses the whole multiplicity

of significative phenomena, whether a knock at the door, a footprint, a spontaneous cry, a painting or a musical score, a conversation, a silent meditation, a piece of writing, a syllogism, an algebraic equation, a geometric diagram, a weather vane, or a simple bookmark. The comparative study of several sign systems carried out by the researcher revealed the fundamental convergences and divergences which had as yet remained unnoticed. Peirce's works demonstrate a particular perspicacity when he deals with the categoric nature of language in the phonic, grammatical and lexical aspects of words as well as in their arrangement within clauses, and in the implementation of the clauses with respect to the utterances. At the same time, the author realizes that his research "must extend over the whole of general Semeiotic," and warns his epistolary interlocutor, Lady Welby: "Perhaps you are in danger of falling into some error in consequence of limiting your studies so much to Language" (Lieb, 1953:39).

Unfortunately most of Peirce's semiotic writings were only published during the fourth decade of our century, i.e. around twenty years after the author's death. Nearly a century was needed to print some of his texts; thus the amazing fragment of one of Peirce's courses given in 1866-67—"Consciousness and Language"—first appeared in 1958 (VII. 579-96); let us note too that there remains in Peirce's heritage numerous unpublished pieces. The tardy publication of his works, which appeared dispersed and in fragments in the maze of the *Collected Papers of Charles Sanders Peirce*, vol. I-VIII, for a long time hampered a complete and exact understanding of his precepts and unfortunately delayed their effective influence on the science of language and the harmonious development of semiotics.

Readers and commentators of these works have often been mistaken about the fundamental terms introduced by

Peirce, although they are indispensable to an understanding of his theory of signs and although these terms, even if forced occasionally, nonetheless receive a definition that is always very clear in the author's text.   Thus the *interpreter* and the *interpretant* designations have given rise to an unfortunate confusion in spite of the distinction Peirce makes between the term *interpreter* which designates the receiver and decoder of a message, and *interpretant*, that is, the key which the receiver uses to understand the message he receives.   According to popularizers, the sole role attributed to the *interpretant* in Peirce's doctrine consists in clarifying each sign by the mediating context, while in fact the brave "pioneer" of semiotics asks rather "to distinguish, in the first place, the Immediate Interpretant, which is the interpretant as it is revealed in the right understanding of the sign itself, and is ordinarily called the *meaning* of the sign" (IV.536).   In other words, it is "all that is explicit in the sign itself, apart from its context and circumstances of utterance" (V.473); all signification is but the "translation of a sign into another system of signs" (IV.127).   Peirce casts light upon the ability of every sign to be translatable into an infinite series of other signs which, in some regards, are always mutually equivalent (II.293).

    According to this theory, the sign demands nothing more than the possibility of being interpreted even in the absence of an addresser.   The symptoms of illnesses are therefore also considered signs (VIII.185, 335) and at a certain point, medical semiology neighbors semiotics, the science of signs.

    In spite of all the differences in the presentation's details, the bipartition of the sign into two conjoined facets and, in particular, the Stoic tradition, which conceives of the sign (σημεῖον) as a referral on the part of the *signans* (σημαῖνον) to the *signatum* (σημαινόμενον), remains strong in Peirce's doctrine.   In conformity with his trichotomy of semiotic modes and with the rather vague names that he gives them, (1) the *index* is a referral from the *signans* to the *signatum* by virtue of an effective contiguity; (2) the *icon* is a referral from the *signans* to the *signatum* by virtue of an effective similarity; (3) the *symbol* is a referral from the *signans* to the *signatum* by virtue of an "imputed," conventional, habitual contiguity. Accordingly (*cf.* in particular II.249, 292 *ff.*, 301, and IV.447 *ff.*, 537), "the mode of being of the symbol is different from that of the icon and from that of the index." In contradistinction to these two categories, the symbol as such is not an object; it is nothing but a frame-rule which must clearly be distinguished from its functioning in the form of "replicas" or "instances," as Peirce tries to define them. The elucidation of the generic character which qualifies both the *signantia* and the *signata* in the code of language (each of these aspects "is a kind and not a single thing") has opened new perspectives on the semiotic study of language.

Now, the trichotomy in question has also given rise to erroneous views. Attempts have been made to attribute to Peirce the idea of the division of all human signs into three rigorously separate classes, while the author only considers three modes, one of which "is predominant over the others" and, in a given system, finds itself often linked to the other two modes or to either of them. For example,

> a symbol may have an icon or an index incorporated into it (IV.447). It is frequently desirable that a repre-sentamen should exercise one of those three functions to the exclusion of the other two, or two of them to the exclusion of the third; but the most perfect of signs are those in which the iconic, indicative, and symbolic characters are blended as equally as possible (IV.448). It would be difficult if not impossible, to instance an absolutely pure index, or to find any sign absolutely

devoid of the indexical quality (II.306). A diagram, though
it will ordinarily have Symbolide Features, as well as
features approaching the nature of Indices, it is nevertheless in the main an Icon (IV.531).

In his successive attempts to establish a complete classification of semiotic phenomena, Peirce ended up outlining a
table consisting of 66 divisions and subdivisions (*cf.* Lieb,
1953:51-53), which embraces the action "of almost any kind
of sign"—action known under the ancient name of σημείωσις.
Ordinary language and the diverse types of formalized languages find their place in Peirce's semiotics which emphasizes
not only the primacy of the symbolic relationship between
the *signans* and the *signatum* in the   linguistic   data   but
at the same time, the co-presence of the iconic and indexical
relationship.

VII

Ferdinand de Saussure's contribution to the progress of
semiotic studies is evidently more modest and more restricted.
His attitude toward the *science de signes* and the name
sémiologie (or sporadically *signologie, cf.* 1974:47 *ff.*)
which he imposed on it immediately, remains, it seems,
completely outside of the current created by such names
as Locke, Lambert, Bolzano, Peirce and Husserl. One can
surmise that he did not even know of their research in semiotics. Nonetheless, in his lessons he asks: "Why hasn't semiotics existed until now?" (1967:52). The question of the
precedent which might have inspired the program con-
structed by Saussure remains unanswered.   His ideas on
the science of signs have only come to us in the form of
sparse notes, the oldest of which date back to the 1890's
(*cf.* Godel, 1957:275), and in the last two of his three

courses in general linguistics (Saussure, 1967:33, 45-52, 153-55, 170 *ff.*).

From the end of the century, Saussure tried to get, according to his own terms, "a correct idea of what a semiological system is" (*cf.* Godel, 1957:49) and to discover the traits "of language, as of the entire general semiologic system" (Saussure, 1954:71), while having in mind mainly systems of "conventional signs." The oldest of Saussure's remarks on the theory of signs try to apply it to the phonic level of language; with a clarity superior to the treatment of the same matter in his later teachings, these theses allow for the emergence of

> the relationship between sound and idea, the semiological value of the phenomenon [which] can and should be studied outside all historical preoccupations, [since] study of the state of language on the same level is perfectly justified (and even necessary, although neglected and poorly understood) insofar as we are dealing with semiologic facts. (cited by Jakobson, 1973:294).

The equation *Phonème=Valeur sémiologique* is placed at the head of the *phonétique sémiologique,* the new discipline foreseen by Saussure at the beginning of his activities at the University of Geneva (*ibid.* 292 and 294).

The only mention of Saussure's semiological ideas that appeared during his lifetime is a brief summary which his relative and colleague, Ad. Naville, gives in a book in 1901 (Chapter 5). The text of the *Cours de linguistique générale,* published in 1916 by Charles Bally and Albert Sechehaye from notes taken by members of Saussure's audience, is so reworked and touched up by the editors that it causes quite a number of errors in the master's teachings. At present, thanks to the beautiful critical edition by Rudolf Engler (1967), we are able to compare the direct accounts of Saussure's students and to get a far truer and far more precise idea of the original text of his talks.

Unlike Peirce and Husserl, who were both conscious of having laid the foundations of semiotics, Saussure speaks of semiotics in the future only. According to the notes on Saussure's courses between 1908 and 1911, which were collected by several students (*cf.* 1967:XI), language is above all a system of signs, and therefore it must be classified as a science of signs (p. 47). This science has hardly developed. Saussure proposes to call it *sémiologie* (from the Greek σημεῖον, *sign*). One cannot say what this science of signs will be, but it is our task to say that it is worthy of existence and that linguistics will occupy the principal compartment of this science; "this will be one particular case of the great semiological fact" (p. 48). Linguists will have to distinguish the semiological characteristics of language in order to place it properly among systems of signs (p.49); the task of the new science will be to bring out the differences between these diverse systems as well as their common characteristics —"There will be general laws of semiology" (p. 47).

Saussure underlines the fact that language is far from being the only system of signs. There are many others: writing, visual nautical signals, military trumpet signals, gestures of politeness, ceremonies, sets of rites (p. 46*sq.*); in the eyes of Saussure, "Customs have a semiological character" (p. 154). The laws of transformation of the systems of signs will have completely topical analogies with language's laws of transformation; and, on the other hand, these laws will reveal enormous differences (pp. 45, 49). Saussure envisions certain dissimilarities in the nature of different signs and in their social value: the personal or impersonal factor, a thought-out act or an unconscious one, dependence or independence vis-à-vis the individual or social will, ubiquity or limitedness. If one compares the different systems of signs with language, one will witness, according to Saussure, the surfacing of aspects which one had not suspected; in studying rites or any other system separately, one will notice that all of these systems yield a common study—that of the specific life of signs, semiology (p. 51).

According to the thesis Saussure maintained from the time of his preparation in 1894 of an unfinished study on William Dwight Whitney (cited by Jakobson, 1973:279 *ff.*), "language is nothing more than one *particular case* of the Theory of Signs," and

> this will be the major reaction of the study of language in the theory of signs, this will be the ever new horizon which it will have opened—to have taught and revealed to the theory of signs *a whole other and new side of the sign,* that is to say that the sign does not begin to be really known until we have seen that it is not only a transmissible thing but by its very nature a thing *destined to be transmitted.*

(therefore, in Peirce's terms, demanding the participation of an "interpreter").

Now, at the same time, Saussure puts the "particularly complex nature of the semiology of spoken language" (*loc. cit.*) in opposition to the other semiological systems. According to the Saussurean doctrine, these systems use signs which have at least a basic link of reference between the *signatum* and the *signans, icons* in Peirce's terminology, *symbols* as Saussure's *Course* will call them later: "The symbol is a sign, but not always completely arbitrary" (1967:155). On the contrary, language is "a system of independent symbols." Thus, in 1894 purely conventional and, as such "arbitrary," signs are those which Peirce called *symbols* (or *legisigns*). "The independent symbols," according to the old notes of Saussure, "possess the particular major characteristic of not having any sort of perceivable connection with the object to be designated." The result is that "whoever sets foot on the terrain of language may say to himself that he is abandoned by all the analogies of heaven and earth" (Jakobson, 1973:153 *sq.*).

Although Saussure is inclined to see the primary concerns of semiology in "arbitrary systems," this science, he affirms, will always see its field grow, and it is difficult to predict where semiology will stop (1967:153 *ff.*). The "grammar" of the game of chess, with the respective value of its pieces, authorizes Saussure to compare game and language and to conclude that in these semiological systems "the notion of identity meshes with that of value, and vice versa" (*ibid.,* 249).

These are precisely the questions linked to identities and values which, according to an astute note made by Suassure at the beginning of the century, appear to be decisive in mythical studies, as in the "parental domain of linguistics": on the level of semiology

> all the incongruities of thought stem from insufficient reflection about what *identity* is, or what the characteristics of identity are, when we talk about a nonexistent being, like a *word*, or a *mythic person*, or *a letter of the alphabet,* which are only different forms of the sign in a philosophical sense.

"These symbols, without realizing it, are subject to the same vicissitudes and to the same laws as are all the other series of symbols . . .—They are all part of semiology" (*cf.* Starobinski, 1971:15). The idea of this semiological being which does not exist *in itself*, "at any time" (*à nul moment*) (1972: 277) is adopted by Saussure in his 1908-09 course where he proclaims "the reciprocal determination of values by their very coexistence," while adding that there are no isolated semiological beings, and that such a determination can occur only on a synchronic level, "for a system of values cannot stay astride a succession of epochs" (*ibid.*, 304).

Saussure's semiotic principles during the last twenty years of his life demonstrate his striking tenacity. The 1894 sketches, cited above, open with an inflexible assertion

> The object that serves as sign is never "the same" (*le même*) twice: one immediately needs an examination or an initial convention to know within what limits and in the name of what we have the right to call it the same; therein lies its fundamental difference from an ordinary object.

These notes insist on the decisive role of the "plexus of eternally negative differences," the ultimate principle of non-coincidence in the world of semiological values. In approaching semiological systems, Saussure tries to "take exception to what preceded," and as of 1894 he gladly refers to comparisons between the synchronic states in language and the chessboard. The question of the "antihistoric character of language" will even serve as title to Saussure's last notes in 1894 (*ibid.*, 282), and, one could add, to all of his thoughts on the semiological aspects of language and of all the *créations symboliques* (*cf.* his notes published by Avalle, 1973:28-38). These are the two intertwined principles of Šaussurean linguistics—*l'arbitraire du signe* and the obstinately "static" conception of the system—which nearly blocked the development of the *sémiologie générale* that the master had foreseen and hoped for (*cf.* Saussure, 1967:170 *ff.*).

Now, the vital idea of semiological invariance which remains valid throughout all of the circumstantial and individual variations is clarified by Saussure thanks to a felicitous comparison of language to the symphony:

the musical work is a reality existing independently of the variety of performances made of it; "the performances do not attain the status of the work itself." "The execution of a sign is not its essential characteristic," as Saussure points out; "the performance of a Beethoven sonata is not the sonata itself" (1967:50, 53 *ff.*). We are dealing with the relationship between *langue* and *parole* and with the analogous link between the "univocality" (*univocité*) of the work and the multiplicity of its individual interpretations. Mistakenly, in the text arranged by Bally and Sechehaye, these [interpretations] are represented as "errors that [the performers] might commit.

Saussure must have thought that in semiology the "arbitrary" signs were going to occupy a fundamental place, but it would be useless to look in his students' notes for the assertion that the Bally-Sechehaye text gives, that is: "signs that are entirely arbitrary actualize the ideal of semiological process better than other signs" (1967:154).

In his expansionist view of the science in the process of becoming (*science en devenir*) Saussure goes as far as to admit that "everything comprising forms must enter into semiology" (*loc. cit.*). This suggestion seems to anticipate the current idea of the topologist Réné Thom (1974) who wonders if one must not immediately attempt to develop a "general theory of forms, independent of the specific nature of substratum space" (p. 244 *ff.*).

VIII

The relationship of the science of language and languages

with that of the sign and of different signs was defined
briefly and explicitly by the philosopher Ernst Cassirer
in his address to the New York Linguistic Circle, pointing
out that "linguistics is a part of semiotics" (1945:115).

There is no doubt that signs belong to a field which is
distinguishable in certain respects from all the other facets
of our environment. All of the sectors of this field need
to be explored, taking into account the generic characteristics and the convergences and divergences among
the various types of signs. Any attempt to tighten the limits
of semiotic research and to exclude from it certain types of
signs threatens to divide the science of signs into two homo-
nymous disciplines, namely *semiotics* in its largest sense
and another province, identically named, but taken it its
narrower sense. For example, one might want to promote
to a specific science the study of signs we call "arbitrary,"
such as those of language (so it is presumed), even
though linguistic symbols, as Peirce demonstrated, can be
easily related to the *icon* and to the *index*.

Those who consider the system of language signs
as the only set worthy of being the object of the science
of signs engage in circular reasoning (*petitio principii*).
The egocentrism of linguists who insist on excluding from
the sphere of semiotics signs which are organized in a different manner than those of language, in fact reduces semiotics to a simple synonym for linguistics. However, the
efforts to restrict the breadth of semiotics go even further
sometimes.

At all levels and in all aspects of language, the reciprocal
relationships between the two facets of the sign, the *signans*
and the *signatum*, remains strong, but it is evident that the
character of the *signatum* and the structuring of the *signans*
change according to the level of linguistic phenomenon. The
privileged role of the right ear (and, more properly, that of

the left hemisphere of the brain) solely in the perception of language sounds is a primary manifestation of their semiotic value, and all the phonic components (whether they are distinctive features, or demarcational, or stylistic, or even strictly redundant elements) function as pertinent signs, each equipped with its own *signatum.* Each level above brings new particularities of meaning: they change substantially by climbing the ladder which leads from the phoneme to the morpheme and from there to words (with all their grammatical and lexical hierarchy), then go through various levels of syntactic structures to the sentence, then to the groupings of sentences into the utterance and finally to the sequences of utterances in dialogue. *Each one* of these successive stages is characterized by its clear and specific properties and by its degree of submission to the rules of the code and to the requirements of the context. At the same time, each part participates, to the extent possible, in the meaning of the whole. The question of knowing what a morpheme means, or what a word, a sentence or a given utterance means, is equally valid for all of these units. The relative complexity of signs such as a syntactic period, a monologue or an interlocution, does not change the fact that in any phenomenon of language everything is a sign. The distinctive features or the whole of a discourse, the linguistic entities, in spite of the structural differences in function and in breadth, all are subject to one common science, the science of signs.

The comparative study of natural and formalized languages, and above all those of logic and mathematics, also belong to semiotics. It is here that the analysis of the various relationships between code and context has already opened broad perspectives. In addition, the confrontation of language with "secondary modeling structures" and with mythology particularly points to a rich harvest and calls upon able minds to undertake an analogous type of work which attempts to embrace the semiotics of culture.

In the semiotic research which touches upon the question of language, one will have to guard against the imprudent application of the special characteristics of language to other semiotic systems. At the same time, one must avoid denying to semiotics the study of systems of signs which have little resemblance to language and following this ostracizing activity to the point of revealing a presumably "non-semiotic" layer in language itself.

IX

Art has long escaped semiotic analysis. Still there is no doubt that all of the arts, whether essentially temporal like music or poetry, or basically spatial like painting or sculpture, or syncretic, spatio-temporal, like theater or circus performances or film showings, are linked to the sign. To speak of the "grammar" of an art is not to employ a useless metaphor: the point is that all art implies an organization of polar and significant categories that are based on the opposition of marked and unmarked terms. All art is linked to a set of artistic conventions. Some are general, for example, let us say that we may take the number of coordinates which serve as a basis for plastic arts and create a consequential distinction between a painting and a piece of statuary. Other conventions, influential ones or even mandatory ones for the artist and for the immediate receivers of his work, are imposed by the style of the nation and of the time. The originality of the work finds itself restricted by the artistic code which dominates at a given epoch and in a given society. The artist's revolt, no less than his faithfulness to certain required rules, is conceived of by contemporaries with respect to the code that the innovator wants to shatter.

The attempted confrontation between arts and language may fail if this comparative study relates to ordinary language and not directly to the verbal art which is a transformed system of the former.

The signs of a given art can carry the imprint of each of the three semiotic modes described by Peirce; thus, they can come near to the *symbol,* to the *icon*, and to the *index,* but it is obviously above all in their artistic characteristic that their significance (σημείωσις) is lodged. What does this particular characteristic consist of? The clearest answer to this question was given in 1885 by a young college student, Gerald Manley Hopkins:

> The artificial part of poetry, perhaps we shall be right to say all artifice, reduces itself to the principle of parallelism. The structure of poetry is that of continuous parallelism (1959:84).

The "artifice" is to be added to the triad of semiotic modes established by Peirce. This triad is based on two binary oppositions: contiguous/similar and factual/imputed. The contiguity of the two components of the sign is factual in the *index* but imputed in the *symbol.* Now, the factual similarity which typifies *icon* finds its logically foreseeable correlative in the imputed similarity which specifies the *artifice* and it is just for this reason that the latter fits into the whole which is now forever a four part entity of semiotic modes.

Each and every sign is a *referral* (*renvoi*) (following the famous *aliquid stat pro aliquo*). The parallelism alluded to by the master and theoretician of poetry, Gerard Manley Hopkins, is a referral from one sign to a similar one in its totality or at least in one of its two facets (the *signans* or the *signatum*). One of the two "correspective" signs, as Saussure designates them (*cf.* Starobinski, 1971:34), refers back to another, present or implied in the same context, as we can see in the case of a metaphor where only the "vehicle" is *in presentia.* Saussure's only finished writing during his professorship in Geneva, a clairvoyant work on the concern for repetition in ancient literatures, would have innovated the world-wide science of poetics, but it was unduly hidden and even today the notebooks, which are quite old, are only known to us through Jean Starobinski's fascinating quotations. This work brings out "the 'coupling,' that is, the repetition in even numbers" in Indo-European poetry which allows for the analysis of "the phonic substance of words whether to construct an acoustical series (e.g. a vowel which requires its 'counter-vowel'), or to make of them a significative series" (*cf.* 1971:21, 31 *ff.*). In trying hard to couple signs which "find themselves naturally evoking each other" (p. 55), poets had to control the traditional "skeleton of the code" and control first the strict rules of approved similarity, including accepted license (or, as Saussure puts it, the "transaction" on certain variables), then the laws prescribed for the even (*paire*) distribution of corresponding units throughout the text and finally the order (*consecutivité* or *non-consecutivité*) imposed on reiterative elements with respect to the march of time (p. 47).

"Parallelism" as a characteristic feature of all artifice is the referral of a semiotic fact to an equivalent fact inside the same context, including the case where the aim of the referral is only an elliptic implication. This infallible belonging of the two parallels to the same context allows us to complement the system of times which Peirce includes in his semiotic triad: "An icon has such being as belongs to past experience . . . An index has the being of present experience. The being of a symbol . . . is

esse in futuro" (IV.447; II.148). The artifice retains the
atemporal interconnection of the two parallels within
their common context.

   Stravinsky (1942) never tired of repeating that "music
is dominated by the principle of similarity." In the musical
art the correspondances of elements that are recognized, in
a given convention, as mutually equivalent or in opposition
to each other, constitute the principal, if not the only, semiotic value—"intramusical embodied meaning," according to
the description by the musicologist Leonard Meyer:

> Within the context of a particular musical style one tone
> or group of tones indicates—leads the practiced listener
> to expect—that another tone or group of tones will be
> forthcoming at some more or less specified point in the
> musical continuum (1967:6 *ff.*)

The referral to what follows is felt by composers as the
essence of the musical sign. In the eyes of Arnold Schönberg,
"to compose is to cast a glance upon the theme's future"
(*cf.* J. Maegaard, 1974). The three fundamental operations
of the musical "artifice"—anticipation, retrospection and
integration—remind us of the fact that it is the study of
melodic phrase undertaken in 1890 by Ehrenfels which
suggested to him not only the notion of "Gestalt," but also
of a precise introduction to the analysis of musical signs:

> In temporal formal qualities only *one* element can, logically,
> be given in [acts of] perceptual representations, while
> the rest are available as images of memory (or as images
> of expectation projected into the future) (p. 263 *ff.*).

If in music the questions of intrinsic relationships prevail
over the tendencies of an iconic order and are capable of
reducing them to nothingness, the representational function

on the other hand, easily comes to the fore in the history of the necessarily spatial visual arts (*cf.* Jakobson, 1973:104 *ff.*). Nonetheless, the existence and the great successes of abstract painting are incontravertible facts. The "responsions" between the various chromatic and geometric categories which, it goes without saying, play a non-prescriptive role in representational painting, become the only semiotic value of abstract painting. The laws of opposition and equivalence which govern the system of the spatial categories that are at work in a painting offer an eloquent example of similarities imputed by the code of the school, of the epoch, of the nation. Now, here, clearly, as is the case in all semiotic systems, the convention is founded on the use and the choice of universally perceptible potentialities.

Instead of the temporal succession which inspires the anticipations and retrospections of the listener of musical phrases, abstract painting makes us aware of a simultaneity of conjoined and intertwined "correspectives." The musical referral which leads us from the present tone to the anticipated or remembered tone is replaced in abstract painting by a reciprocal referral of the factors in question. Here the relationship of the parts and the whole acquires a particular significance, although the idea of the entire work is emphasized in all arts. The manner of being of the parts reveals their solidarity with the whole and it is according to this whole that each of its component parts emerge. This interdependence between the whole and the parts creates a patent referral from the parts to the whole and vice versa. One might recognize in this reciprocal referral a synecdochic procedure, following the traditional definitions of the trope, like that of Isodorus Hispalensis: *"Synecdoche est conceptio, cum a parte totum vel a toto pars intellegitur"* (*cf.* Lausberg, 1960:paragraph 572). In short, significance underlies all the manifestations of the "artifice."

X

By way of concluding, we can propose a tautological formula: Semiotics or, put otherwise, *la science du signe et des signes,* the science of signs, *Zeichenlehre,* has the right and the duty to study the structure of all of the types and systems of signs and to elucidate their various hierarchical relationships, the network of their functions and the common or differing properties of *all* systems. The diversity of the relationships between the code and the message, or between the *signans* and the *signatum* in no way justifies arbitrary and individual attempts to exclude certain classes of signs from semiotic study, as for example non-arbitrary signs as well as those which, having avoided "the test of socialization," remain individual to a certain degree. Semiotics, by virtue of the fact that it is the science of signs, is called upon to encompass *all* the varieties of the *signum.*

Translated from the French
by Patricia Baudoin

References

Avalle, D'Arco Silvio
1973 "La sémiologie de la narrativité chez Saussure", *Essais de la théorie du texte,* Charles Bouazis, ed., (Paris: Editions Galilée).
Benveniste, Emile
1963 *Coup d'oeil sur le développement de la linguistique* (Paris: Académie des inscriptions et belles-lettres).
Bolzano, Bernard
1837 *Wissenschaftslehre. Versuch einer ausführlichen und grösstentheils neuen Darstellung der Logik mit steter Rücksicht auf deren bisherige Bearbeiter* I-IV (Sulzbach: J. E. v. Seidel). Reprint 1930-31 (Leipzig: Felix Meiner, Ed. Wolfgang Schultz).
Braun, Jerzy Bronisław
1969 *Aperçu de la philosophie de Wroński* (Rome: Tip. P. U. G.).
Cassirer, Ernst A.
1945 "Structuralism in Modern Linguistics", *Word* I (Linguistic Circle of New York).
Ehrenfels, Christian von
1890 "Über 'Gestaltqualitäten' ", *Vierteljahrsschrift für wissenschaftliche Philosophie* XIV: 3.
Eisenring, Max E.
1942 *Johann Heinrich Lambert und die wissenschaftliche Philosophie der Gegenwart* (Zurich: Muller, Werder).
Godel, Robert
1957 *Les sources manuscrites du Cours de la linguistique générale de F. de Saussure* (Geneva: Librairie E. Droz).
Hoene-Wroński, J. M.
1897 "Philosophie du langage" *Sept manuscrits inédits*

écrits de 1803 à 1806 (Paris: Au dépot des ouvrages de l'auteur).

Hopkins, Gerard Manley
1959 [1865] "Poetic diction" *The Journals and Papers,* ed. by H. House (London: Oxford University Press).

Husserl, Edmund
1900-01 *Logische Untersuchungen* I-II (Halle a. S.: Niemeyer).
1970 [1890] "Zur Logik der Zeichen (Semiotik)", *Gesammelte Werke* XII (The Hague: Nijhoff).

Jakobson, Roman
1965 "A la recherche de l'essence du langage", *Diogene* LI (Paris).
1973 *Essais de linguistique générale* II (Paris: Editions de Minuit).

Lambert, J. H.
1764 *Neues Organon, oder Gedanken über die Erforschung und Bezeichnung des Wahren und dessen Unterscheidung vom Irrthum und Schein* I, II (Leipzig: Johann Wendler). Reprint 1965: *Philosophische Schriften* I, II (Hindesheim: Georg Olms, ed. Hans-Werner Arndt).

Lausberg, Heinrich
1960 *Handbuch der literarischen Rhetorik* (Munich: Max Hueber).

Lieb, Irwin C.
1953 *Charles S. Peirce's Letters to Lady Welby* (New Haven, Conn.: Whitlocks).

Locke, John
1694 *Essay Concerning Humane Understanding* (London).

Maegaard, Jan
1974 *Studien zur Entwicklung des dodekaphonen Satzes bei Arnold Schönberg* (Copenhagen: W. Hansen).

Meyer, Leonard B.
1967 *Music, the Arts, and Ideas* (Chicago: University of

Chicago Press).

Naville, Adrien
1901 *Nouvelle classification des sciences. Etude philosophique* (Paris: Alcan).

Peirce, Charles Sanders
1931-58 *Collected Papers* I-VIII (Cambridge, Mass.: Harvard University Press). In the references to *Collected Papers* the subdivisions of the text are indicated by Arabic numerals accompanied by the number of the volume in Roman numerals and separated by a period.

Saussure, Ferdinand de
1954 "Notes inédites", *Cahiers Ferdinand de Saussure* XII (Geneva: Librarie E. Droz).
1967, 1974 *Cours de linguistique générale* I, II. Critical edition prepared by Rudolf Engler (Wiesbaden: Otto Harrassowitz).
1972 "Noto sul 'segno' ", ed. by D'Arco Silvio Avalle, *Strumenti critici* XIX (Torino: Einaudi).

Sechehaye, Ch. Albert
1908 *Programme et méthodes de la linguistique théorique* (Paris: Honore Champion).

Starobinski, Jean
1971 *Les mots sous les mots. Les anagrammes de Ferdinand de Saussure* (Paris: Gallimard).

Stravinsky, Igor
1942 *Poétique musicale sous forme de six leçons* (Cambridge, Mass.: Harvard University Press).

Thom, René
1974 "La linguistique, discipline morphologique exemplaire", *Critique* XXX (Paris: Editions de Minuit).

A Few Remarks on Peirce,
Pathfinder in the Science of Language

When pondering a statement by Peirce, one is constantly surprised. What are the roots of his thought? When another's opinion is quoted and reinterpreted by Peirce, it becomes quite original and innovative. And even when Peirce cites himself, he often creates a new idea and he never ceases to strike his reader. I used to say he was so great that no university found a place for him. There was, however, one dramatic exception—the few semesters of Lecturership in Logic at Johns Hopkins. During this period the scholar launched outstanding semiotic ideas in the volume of *Studies in Logic*, edited by him in 1883. There begins his fruitful discussion on the 'universe of discourse', a notion introduced by A. De Morgan and revised and made by Peirce into a gratifying problem for the science of language (see now his *Collected Papers*, 2.517 *ff.*). The same *Studies in Logic* also carried novel views on predication in Peirce's note "The Logic of Relatives" (3.328 *ff.*), in which he wrote:

> A dual relative term, such as "lover" . . . is a common name signifying a pair of objects . . . Every relative has also a *converse*, produced by reversing the order of the members of the pair. Thus, the converse of "lover" is "loved."

It is to the same question of duality, which still preoccupies linguists and semioticians, that Peirce returned in 1899 in discussing with William James the dyadic category of action: "This has two aspects, the Active and the Passive, which are not merely opposite aspects but make relative contrasts between different influences of this Category as More Active and More Passive" (8.315).

At the conclusion of the Bloomington Joint Conference of Anthropologists and Linguists in July 1952 it was said that "one of the greatest pioneers of structural linguistic analysis," Charles Sanders Peirce, not only stated the need for semiotics, but moreover drafted its basic lines. It is his "life-long study of the nature of signs, . . . the work of clearing and opening up" the science of semiotics, "the doctrine of the essential nature and fundamental varieties of possible semiosis" (5.488), and, in this connection, his life-long "careful study of language" (8.287) which enable us to regard Peirce "as a genuine and bold forerunner of structural linguistics." The essential topics of signs in general and verbal signs in particular permeate Peirce's life work.

In a letter of 1905 (8.213) Peirce says:

> On May 14, 1867, after three years of almost insanely concentrated thought, hardly interrupted even by sleep, I produced my one contribution to philosophy in the "New List of Categories" in the Proceedings of the American Academy of Arts and Sciences, Volume VII, pp. 287-298 [see 1.545 *ff.*] . . . We may classify objects according to their matter; as wooden things, iron things, silver things, ivory things, etc. But classification according to STRUC-TURE is generally more important. And it is the same with ideas . . . I hold that a classification of the elements of thought and consciousness according to their formal structure is more important . . . I examine the phaneron and I endeavor to sort out its elements according to the complexity of their structure.

Here from the start we face a clearly structural approach to problems of phenomenology, or in Peirce's terms, 'phaneroscopy' (*cf.* 1.284 *ff.*). In the letter quoted above Peirce adds, "I thus reached my three categories [of signs]." The editor accompanies these words with a footnote: "Peirce then begins a long discussion of the categories and signs," but unfortunately this discussion remains unpublished.

One should not forget that Peirce's life was a most unhappy one. Terrible external conditions, a daily struggle to stay alive, and the lack of a congenial milieu impeded the development of his scientific activities. He died on the eve of the First World War, but only in the early 1930's did his main writings begin to be published. Before then only a few of Peirce's drafts on semiotics were known—the first sketch of 1867, a few ideas outlined during the Baltimore period, and some cursory passages in his mathematical studies—but for the most part his semiotic and linguistic views, elaborated through several decades, especially aroud the turn of the century, remained completely hidden. It is unfortunate that in the great years of scientific fermentation which followed World War I the newly appeared Saussurian *Cours de linguistique générale* could not be confronted with Peirce's arguments: such a match of ideas, both concordant and rival, would perhaps have altered the history of general linguistics and the beginnings of semiotics.

Even when the volumes of Peirce's writings began to appear between the thirties and the fifties, there remained a number of obstacles to a reader's making a close acquaintance with his scientific thought. The "collected papers" contain too many serious omissions. The capricious intermixture of fragments belonging to different periods at times bewilders the reader, especially since Peirce's reflections developed and changed and one would like to follow and delineate the transition of his concepts from the 1860's to our century. The reader is obliged to rework assiduously for himself the whole plan of these volumes in order to get a perspective and to master the whole of Peirce's legacy.

One may quote, for instance, the greatest French linguist of our time, Émile Benveniste, a remarkable theoretician of language. In his paper of 1969, "Sémiologie de la langue," which opened the review *Semiotica,* Benveniste attempted

a comparative evaluation of Saussure and Peirce, the latter
of whom he knew only from his *Selected Writings,* a non-
semiotic anthology compiled by P. P. Wiener in 1958: "En
ce qui concerne la langue, Peirce ne formule rien de précis
ni de spécifique . . . La langue se réduit pour lui aux mots."
However, in reality Peirce spoke on the "importance of mere
words" (3.419), and for him the importance of words arose
from their arrangement in the sentence (4.544) and from the
build-up of propositions. To exemplify the novelty of his
approaches, let us quote at least Peirce's bold reminder that in
the syntax of every language there are logical icons of mimetic
kind "that are aided by conventional rules" (2.281). Admiring
"the vast and splendidly developed science of linguistics"
(1.271), Peirce embraced all the levels of language from
discourse to the ultimate distinctive units and he grasped the
necessity of treating the latter with respect to the relation
between sound and meaning (1.243).

In Peirce's response of 1892 to the English translation
of Lobachevsky's *Geometrical Researches,* which "mark an
epoch in the   history of thought" and which entail "undoubtedly momentous" philosophical consequences, an
autobiographical allusion is obviously hidden: "So long does
it take a pure idea to make its way, unbacked by any interest
more aggressive than the love of truth" (8.91). Precisely
the same may be said about Peirce; many things could have
been understood earlier and more clearly if one had really
known Peirce's landmarks. I must confess that for years I
felt bitterness at being among linguists perhaps the sole
student of Peirce's views. Even the brief remark on semiotics
in Leonard Bloomfield's *Linguistic Aspects of Science* seems
to go back to Charles Morris' commentaries rather than to
Peirce himself.

It should not be forgotten that in Peirce's basic project,
his *System of Logic, from the point of view of Semiotic*
(8.302), he attempted to show "that a Concept is a Sign"
and to define a sign and resolve it "into its ultimate *elements*"

(8.302, 305). For him, semiotics involved a treatment "of the general conditions of signs being signs" and in Peirce's view it was wrong both to confine semiotic work to language and, on the other hand, to exclude language from this work. His program was to study the particular features of language in comparison with the specifics of other sign systems and to define the common features that characterize signs in general. For Peirce, "natural classification takes place by dichotomies" (1.438) and "there is an element of twoness in every set" (1.446). "A *dyad* consists of two *subjects* brought into oneness" (1.326), and Peirce defines the present inquiry as "a study of dyads in the necessary forms of signs" (1.444). He sees language in its formal, grammatical structure as a system of "relational dyads." The essential dyadic relation for Peirce is an opposition; he insisted on "the manifest truth that existence lies in opposition" and declared that "a thing without oppositions *ipso facto* does not exist." According to Peirce, the primary task is to master "the conception of being through opposition" (1.457).

One of the most felicitous, brilliant ideas which general linguistics and semiotics gained from the American thinker is his definition of meaning as "the translation of a sign into another system of signs" (4.127). How many fruitless discussions about mentalism and anti-mentalism would be avoided if one approached the notion of meaning in terms of translation, which no mentalist and no behaviorist could reject. The problem of translation is indeed fundamental in Peirce's views and can and must be utilized systematically. Notwithstanding all the disagreements, misunderstandings, and confusions which have arisen from Peirce's concept of 'interpretants', I would like to state that the set of interpretants is one of the most ingenious findings and effective devices received from Peirce by semiotics in general and by the linguistic analysis of grammatical and lexical meanings in particular. The only difficulty in the use of these tools lies in the obvious need to follow Peirce's careful delimitation of their different types and "to distinguish, in the first place, the Immediate Interpretant, which is the interpretant as it is revealed in the right understanding of the Sign itself, and is ordinarily called the *meaning* of the sign" (4.536): such an interpretant of a sign "is all that is explicit in the sign itself apart from its context and circumstances of utterance" (5.474). One doesn't know a better definition. This 'selective' interpretant, as distinguished from the 'environmental' one, is an indispensable but all too frequently overlooked key for the solution of the vital question of general meanings in the various aspects of verbal and other sign systems.

Peirce belonged to the great generation that broadly developed one of the most salient concepts and terms for geometry, physics, linguistics, psychology, and many other sciences. This is the seminal idea of INVARIANCE. The rational necessity of discovering the invariant behind the numerous variables, the question of the assignment of all these variants to relational constants unaffected by transformations underlie the whole of Peirce's science of signs. The question of invariance appears from the late 1860's in Peirce's semiotic sketches and he ends by showing that on no level is it possible to deal with a sign without considering both an invariant and a transformational variation. Invariance was the main topic of Felix Klein's *Erlanger Program* of 1872 ("Man soll die der Mannigfaltigkeit angehörigen Gebilde hinsichtlich solcher Eigenschaften untersuchen, die durch die Transformationen der Gruppe nicht geändert werden"), and at the same time the necessity of replacing the accidental variants by their "common denominators" was defended by Baudouin de Courtenay in his Kazan lectures. Thus, convergent ideas destined to transform our science, and sciences in general, emerged almost simultaneously. No matter where the model came from, those were timely pursuits for a wide field of research and they are still able to engender new, fruitful interactions between diverse disciplines. In particular, linguistics has very much to learn both from modern topology and from one of Peirce's most fertile semiotic formulations replying to the question of invariance; a symbol "cannot indicate any particular thing; it denotes a kind of thing. Not only that, but it is itself a kind and not a single thing" (2.301); consequently, "the word and its meaning are both general rules" (2.292).

Peirce asks, "How is it possible for an indecomposable element to have any differences in structure?" and answers, "Of internal logical structure it would be clearly impossible," but as to the structure of its possible compounds, "limited differences of structure are possible." He refers to the *groups*, or vertical columns of Mendeleev's table, which "are universally and justly recognized as ever so much more important that the *series*, or horizontal ranks in the same table" (1.289). Thus, in the question of the relation between the components and the compound, Peirce denies (in the same way as the Gestalt psychologists) the possibility of speaking about constituents without analyzing the structural relation between the constituents and the whole. Far from being a mere conglomerate, which Gestaltists labeled *Und-Verbindung,* any whole is conceived of by Peirce as an integral structure. This model remains valid in its dynamic perspective as well. According to fragments of his *Minute Logic,* sketched in 1902 but never completed, "To say that the future does not influence the present is untenable doctrine" (2.86). Here two aspects of causes are distinguished by Peirce: "Efficient causation is that kind of causation whereby the parts compose the whole; final causation is that kind of causation whereby the whole calls out its parts. Final causation without efficient causation is helpless . . . Efficient causation without final causation, however, is worse than helpless, by far: . . . it is blank nothing" (1.220). No such structural classification is possible without taking into account these two copresent and interacting causations.

The most widely known of Peirce's general assertions is that three kinds of signs exist. Yet the things which are best

known quite easily undergo various distortions. Peirce does
not at all shut signs up in one of these three classes. These
divisions are merely three poles, all of which can coexist
within the same sign. The symbol, as he emphasized, may
have an icon and/or an index incorporated into it, and "the
most perfect of signs are those in which the iconic, indicative,
and symbolic characters are blended as equally as possible"
(4.448).

Peirce's definition of the three semiotic 'tenses' was
recently brought to the attention of the astute French
topologist René Thom, who was happy to find here the
solution he himself had strenuously sought for years. Thus,
permit me to conclude my few remarks with this seemingly
entangled, but essentially lucid formula whereby at the
turn of the century Charles Sanders Peirce succeeded in
bridging the chief problems of semiotics and grammar:

> Thus the mode of being of the symbol is different from
> that of the icon and from that of the index. An icon has
> such being as belongs to PAST experience . . . An index
> has the being of PRESENT experience. The being of a
> symbol consists in the real fact that something will be
> experienced if certain conditions be satisfied [4.447].—It
> is a potentiality: and its mode of being is *esse in futuro*.
> The FUTURE is potential not actual [2.148].—The value
> of an icon consists in its exhibiting the features of a state
> of things regarded as if it were purely imaginary. The
> value of an index is that it assures us of positive fact. The
> value of a symbol is that it serves to make thought
> and conduct rational and enables us to predict the future
> [4.448].

The predominant task of symbols in our verbal (and
not only verbal) creativity could be considered the main-
spring of Peirce's doctrine, but I hate to use the label 'doctrine', for the thinker himself categorically declared that for
him science was not doctrine, but inquiry.

Glosses on the Medieval Insight into the Science of Language*

Benveniste's succinct survey of recent tendencies in general linguistics underscores "le caractère exclusivement historique qui marquait la linguistique pendant tout le XIXe siècle et le début du XXe" (Benveniste, 1954). One would think that this rigorously historical treatment of language, particularly stern in the leading linguistic current of the late nineteenth century, might have generated a thoroughly historical approach to the science of language as well. If, however, this school proved unable to produce a comprehensive history of linguistics, the reason lies in the erroneous reduction of linguistic science to historical or, properly speaking, genealogical questions and in the subsequent

---

*Mélanges Linguistiques offerts à Émile Benveniste (Paris, 1975).

conclusion that the history of scientific linguistics begins only with the first scholarly endeavors to cope with such kinds of tasks.

The broad and durable popularity of the mentioned tenet has resulted in the ingrained and widespread belief that linguistics belongs to the young, even to the youngest sciences, whereas the very antithesis has to be expressly stated. The science of language is one of the oldest, perhaps even the oldest branch of systematic knowledge, or, according to the reiterated Scholastic adages, *scientia linguae est prima naturaliter* and *ceterarum omnium artium nutrix antiquissima.* Any pattern of writing, whether logographic, syllabic, or by and large alphabetic, is in itself a display of linguistic analysis. The earliest extant attempt toward a grammatical parsing and description, namely an outline of Sumerian grammar dating back almost four millennia and investigated by Thorkild Jacobsen (1974), is a remarkable Babylonian effort to cope with the knotty paradigm problem which, in fact, still pertains to the fundamentals of linguistic science.

The pristine origin of linguistic science is quite explicable. Language when used to talk about language is labeled metalanguage; linguists' discourse about language is an elaborate implementation of metalanguage, and since, moreover, any child's progressive acquisition of language is indispensibly joined with mastering the use of metalanguage, such primordial deliberations on language favor and further the emergence of a genuine inquiry into the verbal code.

Linguistics of today effectively combines and brings into concord innovations with an agelong and ever vital tradition of research and argumentation. Only a superstitious belief in a rectilinear progress of science would call into question the evident fact that any temporary current of linguistic thought is ·oriented toward certain angles of language and that in their investigation such a trend uses a restricted number of favorite contrivances. Under those circumstances, some targets and approaches remain in the shadow, as long as the inquirer does not gain a widened scope and deeper insight by familiarizing himself with questions and working hypotheses raised in linguistics of the near and remote past and by testing them on the rich material gathered and accumulated since. One may quote the great musical reformer of our century: according to Igor Stravinsky, "a *renewal* is fruitful only when it goes hand in had with *tradition*. Living dialectic wills that renewal and tradition shall develop and abet each other in a simultaneous process" (Stravinsky, 1947).

A fancy kind of antitraditionalism is verily a traditional feature in the history of linguistic science. Jespersen's incisive remark on neo-grammarians of the eighties could be equally applied to various turns of time: while the ablest linguists of the new school "were taking up a great many questions of vast general importance that had not been treated by the older generation [or rather generations], on the other hand they were losing interest in some of the problems that had occupied their predecessors"; some of these issues went "out of fashion" and were "deprecated" as "futile and nebulous" (Jespersen, 1922). Discoveries and oblivions are used to go together, and some transient losses of remembrance may become an experimental asset. Beside the alternation of attractions and repulsions there exists, however, the beneficial phenomenon of synthesis, devoid of any miscarrying eclecticism, and our days seem to develop a particular aptitude for such a higher dialectic stage.

The use of preconceived and hackneyed schemes for the delineation of the bygone epochs and schools proves to be the greatest stumbling block on the way to an objective historical view of linguistics from the ancient times until recent decades. Too often polemic slogans used by the younger scholarly teams in order to dissociate their aspirations from the precepts of the older generation are substituted

for independent studies and unbiased interpretations of
its bequest.

Thus, for instance, the still current allegation of linguistics manuals that the science of language did not advance
in the Middle Ages is a mere proofless repetition of Humanist
invectives *contra modos significandi.* In reality, one could
easily assert, with particular reference to Jan Pinborg's
expert compendium (1967), and several other historical
surveys—by P. Rotta (1909), R. H. Robins (1951), P. A.
Verburg (1952), B. E. O'Mahony (1964), E. Coseriu (1969),
G. L. Bursill-Hall (1971), and J. Stéfanini (1973)—as well
as to those, still too few, of the numerous manuscript treatises which so far have been published, that throughout the
Middle Ages linguistic analysis was in the focus of acute
scholarly attention, and especially the studies of the so-
called *modistae* and of their precursors underwent in the
period from the late twelfth till the early fourteenth century
a strenuous and diversified development.

The sphere of lexical meanings (*significata dictionum
specialia*) was accurately discriminated from the system of
grammatical meanings (*significata generalia*). The focal
point of those Schoolmen's research, *modi significandi,*
or in modern, Sapirian terminology, "grammatical concepts"
(Sapir, 1921), were submitted to an ever stricter definition
and examination of their specifics and hierarchical interrelation, with a particular attention paid to the parts of
speech (*modi significandi essentiales*) and to their categorial
modifications, such as cases or tenses (*modi significandi
accidentales* with further subdivisions). Sapir's preliminaries
to a classification of the parts of speech (1930) are reminis-
cent of the medieval endeavors to define them strictly
modaliter.

In the analysis into *modi significandi* and their *differ-
entiae specificae* every part of speech appears as a bundle
of elementary features and each of these minimal differential
features is termed and interpreted by Simon Dacus (*cf.* Otto,

1963) and Siger de Cortraco (*cf.* Wạllerand, 1913:10) as *modus significandi specificus.* Thus all *appellativa,* viz. substantive and adjective nouns jointly with substantive and adjective pronouns, signify *per modum entis,* in contradistinction to the *modus esse* of the verbal class. As it was elucidated by Petrus Hispanus, *nomen est vox singificantiva ad placitum sine tempore,* in opposition to the temporal axis which marks the verb (Bocheński, 1947 and Mullally, 1945). The adjective class of nouns and pronouns is separated from the substantive class of these two categories by the *modus adiacentis* opposed to the *modus per se stantis,* while the substantive and adjective nouns by their *modus determinatae apprehensionis* stand in opposition to the *apprehensio indeterminata* of the substantive and adjective pronouns. Authors of treatises *de modis significandi* may differ in terminological and definitional details, but in essence they follow the same principles of classification.

The corollary from such study of the *partes orationis in habitu,* viz. in the paradigmatic interralation, was within the *Summa grammaticae* the systematic inquiry into *partes orationis in actu,* namely into the rules (*canones* or *regulae*) of their interconnection (*congruitas*) in binary syntactic structures, tersely defined as *congrua constructibilium unio ex modo significandi causata* (see de Rijk, 1956:53 and Thurot, 1868:219). The formation of such "unions" or *principia constructionis,* in terms of the "Questiones de modis significandi" written by Nicolaus de Bohemia toward 1300 (Pinborg, 1967:100), underwent a close scrutiny and notable methodological deliberations. Consistent efforts to classify the diverse couples of *constructibilia,* as shown by Johannes de Rus in his *Tractatus de constructione* of the mid-thirteenth century (Pinborg, 1967:52), mark a new stage of syntactic analysis.

The different levels of linguistic phenomena were clearly discerned. The sound of the word (*vox significativa audita*) and its meaning (*significatio vero vel intellectus*)

are opposed to each other as *principium formale dictionis.*
The notion of double articulation echoed nowadays in Russian and thereupon in Western linguistics may be traced back
to the *doctrina de modis significandi* with its clear-cut
idea of *articulatio prima et secunda,* which emerged perhaps
under Greek incentives: one of these two articulations turns
the sound matter (*vocis articulatio*) into words, while the
other employs words to generate sentences (*cf.* Grabmann,
1956:234 and Pinborg, 1967:44).

Each linguistic level obtains an adequate portrayal. Thus
a proficient classifier of the thirteenth century, Guillelmus de
Shyreswoode (Grabmann, 1937), scrupulously delineates
the speech sounds:

> *Sonus unus vox, alius non vox. Sonus vox est ut quod*
> *fit ab ore aminalis; sonus non vox ut strepitus pedum,*
> *fragor arborum et similia.*
>
> *Vox sic dividitur: alia significativa, alia non significativa.*
> *Vox significativa est, quo aliquid significat, non signifi-*
> *cativa, que nil significat ut buba blictrix.*
>
> *Vox significativa quedam significat naturaliter, quedam*
> *ad placitum. Naturaliter, que natura agente aliquid signi-*
> *ficat ut gemitus infirmorum et similia; ad placitum, que*
> *ex humana institutione significationem recipit.*

In a similar way *significatio* is defined by Petrus Hispanus
(Bocheński, 1947): *rei per vocem secundum placitum*
repraesentatio.

On the threshold of our century the second volume
of Husserl's *Logical Investigations* (1901), and especially its chapter "Der Unterschied der selbständigen
und unselbständigen Bedeutungen und die Idee der
reinen Grammatik" which soon became one of the milestones
for the initial advance of structural linguistics, counter-
posed to the current, "exclusively empirical" grammar
the early and once again timely "idea of a general and,
particularly, a priori grammar". He proclaimed "the
indubitably righteous design of a universal grammar as

conceived by the rationalism of the seventeenth and eight-
eenth centuries". As Anton Marty, near to Husserl's train of
thought, states in his lifework on the theory of language
(Marty, 1908:33), a "quite valuable contribution to general
grammar" was made not only by Cartesians, but also by the
third book of Locke's *Essay* (1690) and by the *Nouveaux
essais* of Leibniz (1703), and the idea of a reasoned, general,
universal grammar is to be traced even farther back, particularly to the Stoics and Scholastics. The connection of
Husserl's acute insight into the phenomenology of language
with the medieval philosophy of verbal signification has been
pointed out (Kukenheim, 1962).

The pattern of grammar cherished, elaborated, and
propagated by the *modistae* was *grammatica rationalis,* which
they appraised as the purely and thoroughly scientific view
of language, a *scientia speculativa* (Pinborg, 1969:18), in
contradistinction to the merely applied character of the so-
called *grammatica positiva* or *practica.*

In his theory of verbal symbols and of signs in general
Charles Sanders Peirce, as he himself acknowledges, "derived
the greatest advantage from a deeply pondering perusal of
some of the works of Medieval thinkers" and her refers
expressly to Petrus Abaelardus with his younger contemporary Johannes de Salisbury, and to such eminent Schoolmen
of the thirteenth century as Guillelmus de Shyreswoode and
Petrus Hispanus (Peirce, 1931:1.560, 2.317, 2.486). But
the chief scholastic impetus for Peirce and for later theoreticians of language (*cf.* Heidegger, 1916 and Werner, 1877)
was *Grammatica speculativa,* long attributed to Johannes
Duns Scotus, but actually written at the beginning of the
fourteenth century by Thomas de Erfordia (Bursill-Hall,
1972), an astute and successful compiler of earlier theses
de modis significandi (Pinborg, 1967:134). Peirce, as he
himself says, shared the aim of this work from his own first
steps in the late sixties toward a "general theory of the
nature and meanings of signs", a science he even called

"speculative grammar" before adopting Locke's term "semiotic" (Peirce, 1931:1.445, 2.83, 2.332, *cf.* Jakobson, 1973).

The medieval contributors to the development of scientific, rational grammar particularly insisted on the idea of *grammatica universalis*. The heightened interest in general rules and properties must have been spurred by the vehement sway of Arabic linguistic thought (Pinborg, 1967:25) and put a particular emphasis upon the invariants, for *in his impermutabilibus consistit grammatica regularis,* as it was taught since the early thirteenth century. Pursuit of universals met with mutually parallel problems on different levels of language, and the inquiry into those principles of syntactic constructions which *eadem sunt apud omnes* implied an intrinsic analysis of the *constructibilia* or, in other words, a search for the fundamentals (*generates virtutes*) of the *modi significandi* as such. Neither the question of general rules on the level of *voces significativae,* nor their essential affinity with the *principia generalia* on the higher levels of language were overlooked by the outliners of the *grammatica universalis.* One of the most sagacious medieval linguists, Robertus Kilwardby of the mid-thirteenth century, whose precious manuscripts are still waiting for publication and for a comprehensive interpretation, expressly states that *modi pronuntiandi substantiales elementorum . . . et similiter modi significandi et consignificandi generales* are identical *apud omnes* (Thurot, 1868:125); and the example both he and Nicolaus de Parisiis refer to, the "necessary" and world-wide functional distinction between vowels and consonants (*omnis vocalis per se sonat, consonans cum alio*), reappears in a quite analogous, rigorously distributional formulation used by the recent glossematic doctrine.

The oscillating attitudes observable among the adherents of universal grammar in regard to the diversity of linguistic structures and to their peculiarities *apud gentem illam cuius est lingua* led in the thirteenth century to a heated argument. In Kilwardby's creed, which enriches the long history of those adhesive ideas the recur again and again, the "deep structure", as it would be labeled today, can and must be abstracted by the grammarian *ab omni lingua*, and the elicited product of this operation, the universally compulsory *sermo significativus* may be present *in mente* solely (Pinborg, 1967:29). Or, in a somewhat later response of Boethius Dacus, *non enim omnia possibilia sunt in actu* (Pinborg, 1969:160, 201).

In accordance with patristic philosophy, medieval theoreticians of language paid rapt attention to internal speech, termed *verbum mentis sive interius* by Thomas Aquinas (Manthy, 1937), *sermo interior* by Occam, for whom *triplex est terminus: scriptus, prolatus*, and *conceptus*, more exactly defined as *intentio* and as *pars propositionis mentalis* (Boehner, 1954-1957). Later this vital aspect of language remained underrated or unnoticed for a long span of time.

Boethius Dacus, who during the 1270s taught at the Faculty of Arts in the University of Paris (Jensen, 1963), is perhaps the most original and radical mind not only within the glorious group of Parisian scholars *de Dacia* in the late thirteenth century (*cf.* Otto, 1955, 1963 and Roos, 1961), but also among all medieval inquirers into *modi significandi*. He was one of the greatest Danish contributors to the theory of language, and we do not forget that it was Denmark which throughout many centuries gave to international linguistics a long list of supreme thinkers. The consistently elaborated doctrine of Boethius (Pinborg, 1969) faces us once more with those urgent themes and pointed claims which steadily recur on the winding paths of our science. Throughout the late twelfth and the following century we observe a gradual emancipation of linguistics. The first stage, as noted by Pinborg, was a progressing separation of grammar, concerned with *sermo congruus,* from logic whose subject matter, *sermo verus,* was declared irrelevant for the science of language. The initial advances toward such a bifurcation were made in the twelfth century by Hugo de Sancto Victore (Hunt, 1948:99 *ff.*) and consolidated by the *modistae* of the early thirteenth century. The next resolute step intended to free the science of grammar from all extraneous controlling influences was taken by Boethius Dacus. This scholar's methodological requirement for the elicitation of any scientific, and specifically grammatical theme always and solely *ex principis suae scientiae* underlies and determines his whole treatment of grammatical concepts.

According to Boethius' doctrine (*cf.* Pinborg, 1967: 78-85) the *modi significandi* pertain to the realm of *signa* or, in a closer view, linguistic signs, and nothing outside of this sphere—neither *res,* nor *modi essendi*—enters into the scope of grammarian's competence. The combination of two meanings—one lexical, and the other grammatical—within a word is an inherent and creative capability of language. Thus, for example, a substantive does not name a substance but shows only that the given *conceptus mentis* is represented like a substance (*per modum substantiae*) yet could be actually represented by any other part of speech (*idem conceptus mentis per omnes partes orationis potest significari*), and on the other hand, everything, whether an actual entity or a negation a pure figment, in its linguistic expression may obtain *modum significandi essentialem nominis*. Hence all such words become genuine substantives, irrespective of their lexical meanings (*singificata lectionum*).

The insistence upon the creative power of language, which is peculiar to the whole movement of *modistae*, appears particularly outspoken in Boethius Dacus and somewhat differently in Raymundus Lullus with his conception of language as *ars inveniendi* (Verburg, 1952:54 *ff.*). This resolute emphasis shows homologous features with the powerful poetic trend which enveloped the various countries of Europe precisely through the late twelfth and most of the thirteenth century and which displayed an intent concentration on the inner creativity of verbal art. In a brief commentary to the so-called "parabolic-figurative style" cherished during that epoch in Russia, I was faced with such striking parallels as "the Golden Age of the French medieval literature" with its meridional *poésie récluse* (Provençal *trobar clus*) of Raimbaut d'Aurenga and Arnaud Daniel de Ribérac, or the German *blüemen* in Wolfram's epics. Among further "synchronic international correspondences", one had to evoke the subtle symbolism and hermetism cultivated in the scaldic poetry of the late twelfth century, similar tendencies in the ˇIrish poetry of the same time, enigmatic speech (*significatio*) and *ornatus difficilis* advocated in the contemporaneous Latin manuals of *ars poetica,* especially by Ganfredus de Vinosalvo, and practiced in the international Latin poetry after the First Crusade, and finally the same epoch in the Byzantine literary mastery with its "multiplex semantic structures" (Jakobson, 1952).

Conspicuous affinities between verbal art and verbal theory are a noteworthy and periodically reemerging phenomenon. A historical confrontation of Old Indic poetry and equally subtle treatises on poetic form with the native science of language would undoubtedly throw a new light on many cruxes of Sanskrit poetics and linguistics. We recall Saussure's stirring suspicion of an influence which the traditional analytic devices practiced in Vedic carmina might have exerted upon the grammatical science of India, "au double point de vue *phonique* et *mophologique*" (Starobinski, 1971:38).

Returning to the deliberations of medieval linguists, I must confess that the more one is plunged in their writings, the stronger is the impression of an unsurpassed skill in the arduous tasks of semantic theory. If Boethius Dacus and the other investigators of the *modi significandi* have taken the first place in unraveling the complexity of GRAMMATICAL meanings, the other influential course of medieval thought deeply concerned with language, namely the theory of *suppositiones* [surveyed by Arnold (1952), but still waiting for a systematic linguistic interpretation and apprisal] (*cf.* de Rijk, 1971), give us the firmest outlook on multiple questions tied to LEXICAL meanings and especially on the cardinal problem of general and contextual meanings in their hierarchical relationship. The question of "congruous speech" plays a focal role in the study of the *modi significandi*, while problems of "intelligible speech" become prime in the analysis of the *suppositiones*.

In an effort to disentangle the intricate questions of lexical meaning and to find the way to their persuasive solution, K. O. Erdmann published a paper on the system of "suppositions" as one of the crucial topics of Scholastic preoccupations with thought and language in their interplay, and later, in 1900, changed this essay into a chapter of his book *Die Bedeutung des Wortes* (Erdmann, 1900):

> *Die Lehre der Supposition, die Jahrhunderte hindurch in unerhörter Breite ausgesponnen wurde, ist heute so gut wie vergessen. Der Begriff der Supposition selbst sollte nicht vergessen werden: er umfasst un kennzeichnet eine Gruppe wichtiger Tatsachen.*

Peirce insisted on reviving the concept and name of suppositions and on pursuing the relevant distinction between "signification" and "supposition" (Peirce, 1931: 5.320): *Differunt autem significatio et suppositio*—as it has been stated by Petrus Hispanus—*unde signification prior est suppositione* (Bocheński, 1947). From the twelfth century on, the perplex phenomenon of *univocatio* was defined and treated as *manente eadem significatione variata nominis suppositio* (Arnold, 1952:60).

According to Peirce, "nothing can be clearer" than the thesis he liked to quote from the *Metalogicon* II of Johannes de Salisbury (Peirce, 1931:2.317, 2.364, 2.391, 2.434): *Aliud scilicet esse quod appellativa significant et aliud esse quod nominant. Nominantur singularia sed universalia significantur* (*cf.* Webb, 1929). The dialectical tension between the generic unity of the inherent meaning, on the one hand, and the multitude of contextual meanings, *suppositionum varietas,* on the other hand, or briefly, between intension (depth) and extension (breadth), was conceived as the fundamental *proprietas terminorum.* The manifold adaptations of inherent meanings to diverse types of verbalized or verbalizable contexts was turned by Schoolmen, from Petrus Abaelardus (de Rijk, 1963) and Petrus Helias (Hunt, 1950) to Guillelmus Occam (Boehner, 1957 and Moody, 1935), into shrewd stemmata ("trees") with dichotomously systematized types of suppositions (*cf.* Arnold, 1952:109 and Bursill-Hall, 1971:348 *ff.*) The ways in which *per translationem* a *nomen* turns in discourse into a *terminus* were intently explored, with many still valid and suggestive linguistic finds, and with a rigid delimination of *suppositio formalis* (object language) and different varieties of *suppositio materialis* (metalanguage), neatly discerned by Shyreswoode (Grabmann, 1937).

A shaken but nonetheless tenacious prejudice incessantly attributes to the Middle Ages a plain ignorance of linguistic science. This bias shows to how great an extent we remain ignorant even in the cornerstones of medieval thought which, as a matter of fact, obviously outdate some new-day preliminaries to the theory and methodology of semantics.

Nevertheless, the abundant examples of gratuitous oblivion and presumptuous contempt cannot obliterate the fact of the latent and intermittent but still fertile continuity. On the one hand, the Schoolmen's linguistic tenets had been nursed by Greek and Latin antiquity, in particular by the Aristotelian and Stoic thought with the latter's Augustinian sequel, and by Donatus and Priscianus, the renowned transmitters of Alexandrian models. Also Patristic and Byzantine (*cf.* Anderson, 1973), as well as Arabic cogitations seem to have impelled the Western medieval inquirers into language.

On the other hand, the Scholastic search left deep, though mostly hidden traces in the grammatical theories of the later centuries. First and foremost one may cite such a landmark in the development of the *scientia linguae* as the greatest achievement of Renaissance linguistics, the book by Franciscus Sanctius Brocensis, *Minerva: seu de causis linguae Latinae* (or, according to another variant of the subtitle: *sive de proprietate sermonis Latini*) (Sanctius, 1562; cf. Liaño Pacheco, 1971) with its leading principle—*syntaxis est finis grammaticae*—and with a stupendous series of conjugate chapters, "*De ellipsi*", "*De zeugmate*", and "*De vocibus homonymis*" All three of them were apparently stimulated by the *Syntaxis figurata* which Thomas Linacer had offered at the end of his renowned syntactic manual in accordance with a time-honored compositional pattern (Linacer, 1524). *Minerva,* imbued with the idea of ellipticity as the motive power of language, is firmly rooted in the foundations of the Schoolmen's *grammatica rationalis* and in the medieval manuals of rhetoric (which unfortunately remain even less explored than their grammatical counterparts). At the same time this bold "Cathedratico de Rhetorica en Salamanca", with his emphasis upon a strictly rational method (*ratio* opposed to *auctoritas*) and upon a critical approach to the ruling of *magni viri,* has been rightly considered a "precursor of rationalism" and a discoverer of novel linguistic paths and prospects (Navarro Funes, 1929; Garcia, 1960; Lázaro Carreter, 1949; Estal Fuentes, 1973).

His work enjoyed a widespread popularity; between 1664 and the beginning of the nineteenth century it was printed, with retouches and additions by commentators, at least twelve times in various European centers. As early as 1628, one of these enrapt commentators, Gasper Scioppius, published his own *Grammatica philosophica,* centered around ellipsis and opening the way to many successive samples of tentative "philosophical grammars". In the nineteenth century, despite the hostility of the sectarian historicism toward the fanatic seeker of ellipsis, rare instances of deserved recognition still emerged and Sanctus was even hailed as Humboldt's precursor by a grammarian of

Humboldtian stamp (Michelsen, 1837). Through the 1870's and 80's, in an international linguistic and philosophical discussion upon the very essence of impersonal sentences, their three-centuries-old elliptic interpretation by Sánchez de las Brozas was still cited and reinterpreted (Miklosich, 1883).

In the past century the distinguished Italian critic Francesco de Sanctis proclaimed Sánchez Brocense "the Descartes of Grammarians". Benedetto Croce recalls this appraisal and views the Spanish savant as the most profound among the Renaissance explorers of language (Croce, 1902). Since the beginning of our century there has grown both in Spain and in international scholarship a new attraction toward *Minerva's* linguistic anticipations which are cognate both with the Schoolmen's legacy and with the modern scientific quest. Golling's "Introduction in the the History of Latin Syntax" (Golling, 1903:52 *ff.*) declared in 1903:

> *Die glänzendste Erscheinung unter den Grammatikern des 16. und der beiden folgenden Jahrhunderte is Fr. Sanctius Brocensis. In seiner* Minerva *sucht er . . . die innere Notwendigkeit und logische Geschlossenheit der lateinischen Syntax nachzuweisen . . . Der tiefe spekulative Blick verbunden mit logischer Schärfe und Konsequenz [hat] dem Sanctius eine Bedeutung verliehen, die seine Lehren noch in der Gegenwart als beachtenswert erscheinen lässt.*

In the grammatical literature of the seventeenth century the place of prominence belongs to Arnauld's and Lancelot's *Grammaire générale et raisonnée,* which aimed to explain, as the subtitle claims, "les raisons de ce qui est commun à toutes les langues et des principales différences qui s'y rencontrent". This significant work and its governing methods and principles, as it was clearly and decisively stated by Claude Lancelot, the experienced linguistic coeditor of the Port-Royal publication, obviously depend on the hundred-years older *Minerva*. The latter was the main, but certainly the only guide through which Scholastic approaches to grammatical problems pervaded "les fondemens de l'art de parler" of the Port-Royal team. The diffusion of the *Grammaire générale et raisonnée*, whether direct or mediate, since its original edition of 1660, was enormous until the first half of the last century, a century which after 1846 put an end to its numerous republications. The temporary aversion and oblivion, linked to the one-sided historical bent which was particularly potent among linguists of the late nineteenth century, found, however, a severe retort in Saussure's *Course of General Linguistics*, recorded by his students (Saussure, 1967:183 *ff.*):

> *La base de la grammaire de Port Royal était beaucoup plus scientifique que celle de la linguistique postérieure . . . . Après avoir fait de l'histoire linguistique fort longtemps, il est certain qu'il faudra revenir sur la grammaire statique traditionnelle, mais y revenir avec un point de vue renouvelé . . . . Ce sera une des utilités de l'étude historique d'avoir fait comprendre ce qu'était un état. La grammaire traditionnelle ne s'est occupée que de faits statiques; "la linguistique historique" nous a fait connàitre un nouvel ordre de faits, mais ce que nous disons: ce n'est que l'opposition des deux ordres qui est féconde comme point de vue.*

Saussure countered the neogrammarian negative attitude toward the Port Royalists by a negation of negation, and his inerrable flair for the dialectic of scientific advance confronts us with a predictable continuation of this development in the recent fierce discussions, reevaluations, and critical editions of this "traditional" textbook (see Chomsky, 1966; Aarsleff, 1970; Brekle, 1966; Lakoff, 1969; Arnauld, 1969 and Hall, 1969 for further bibliography). One could again recall Stravinsky's catchword on renewal and tradition, which "develop and abet each other in a simultaneous process".

References

Aarsleff, H.
 1970 "The History of Linguistics and Prof. Chomsky",
       Language, 46.
Anderson, J. M.
 1973 "Maximi Planudis in Memoriam", *Generative
       Grammar in Europe,* Ed. by F. Kiefer & N. Ruwet.
Arnauld, A. & C. Lancelot
 1969 *Grammaire générale et raisonée,* avec les remarques
       de C. P. Duclos, préface de M. Foucalt (Paris).
Arnold, E.
 1952 "Zur Geschichte der Suppositionstheorie", *Sym-
       posion,* III (Munich).
Bel, A. F. G.
 1925 *Francisco Sánchez el Brocenese* = *Hispanic Notes &
       Monographs Issued by the Hispanic Society of
       America,* VII (London).
Benveniste, É.
 1954 "Tendences récentes en linguistique genérale",
       JPs 47-51, 103-145 (= *PLG* 1, 3-17).
 1967 "La forme et les sens dans le langage", *La langage:
       Actes du XIIIe Congrès des societés de philosophie
       de langue française,* II:29-40 (Neuchâtel) (= *PLG*
       2, 215-218).
Bocheński, J. M.
 1947 *Summulae Logicales Petri Hispani* (Rome).
Boehner, P. (ed.)
 1954-57 *Geuillelmus Ockham, Summa logicae* = *Fran-
       ciscan Institute Publications,* Text series, II.
Brekle, H. H. (ed)
 1966 *Grammaire générale et raisonnée, ou La grammaire
       du Port Royal,* I-II (Stuttgart).
Bursill-Hall, G. L. (ed.)
 1971 *Speculative Grammars in the Middle Ages* (The
       Hague-Paris).
 1972 *Thomas of Erfurt: Grammatica speculativa* (London).

Chomsky, Noam
1966 *Cartesian Linguistics* (New York & London).
Coseriu, E.
1969 *Die Geschichte der Sprachphilosophie von der Antike bis zur Gegenwart,* I (Stuttgart).
Croce, B.
1902 *Estetica come scienza dell' espressione e linguistica generale* (Palermo).
Erdmann, K. O.
1900 *Die Bedeutung des Wortes* (Leipzig).
Estal Fuentes, E. del
1973 *Francisco Sánchez de las Brozas y la doctrina de la elipsis. Introducción al estudio de la Minerva,* Facultad de Filosofia y Letras (Salamanca).
Garcia, C.
1960 "Contribución a la historia de los cenceptos grammaticales. La aportación del Brocense", *Revista de Filologia Española,* 71 (Madrid).
Golling, J.
1903 "Einleitung in die Geschichte der lateinschen Syntax", *Historische Grammatik der lateinischen Sprache,* ed. G. Landgraf, III (Leipzig).
Grabmann, M.
1926 "Die Entwicklung der mittelalterlichen Sprachlogik (Tractatus de modis significandi)", *Mittelalterliches Geistesleben,* I (Munich).
1937 "Die Introductiones in logicam des Wilhelm von Shyreswood", *Sitzungsberichte der Bayerischen Akademie der Wissenschaften,* Heft X.
1956 "Der Kommentar des seligen Jordanus von Sachsen zum Priscianus minor", *Mittelalterliches Geistesleben* (Munich).
"Die geschichtliche Entwicklung der mittelalterlichen Sprachphilosophie und Sprachlogik", *ibidem.*
Hall, R. A., Jr.
1969 "Some Recent Studies on Port-Royal and Vaugelas", *Acta Linguistica Hafniensia,* 12.

Heidegger, M.
1916 *Die Kategorien- und Bedeutungslehre des Duns Scotus* (Tübingen).
Hunt, R. W.
1941-43 "Studies on Priscian in the Twelfth Century", *Mediaeval and Renaissance Studies*, I.
1950 Ibid., *Mediaeval and Renaissance Studies*, II.
1948 "The Introductiones to the 'Artes' in the Twelfth Century", *Studia mediaevalia in honorem R. J. Martin* (Brugge).
Husserl, E.
1901 *Logische Untersuchungen*, II (Halle). See also 1913 edition.
Jacobsen, T.
1974 "Very Ancient Linguistics", *Studies in the History of Linguistics*, ed. by Dell Hymes (Bloomington: Indiana University Press).
Jakobson, R.
1952 "The Puzzles of the Igor' Tale", *Speculum*, 27.
1973 *Main Trends in the Science of Language* (London).
Jensen, S. S.
1963 "On the National Origin of the Philosopher Boetius de Dacia", *Classica et Mediaevalia*, 24.
Jespersen, O.
1922 *Language, Its Nature, Development and Origin* (London).
Kukenheim, L.
1962 *Esquisse historique de la linguistique française et de ses rapports avec la linguistique générale* (Leiden).
Kuroda, S.-Y.
1972 "Anton Marty and the Transformational Theory of Language", *Foundations of Language*, 9.
Lakoff, Robin
1969 Review of Brekle (1966) in *Language*, 45:343-364.
Lázaro Carreter, C. F.
1949 *Las ideas lingüísticas en Espana durante el siglo XVIII* (Madrid).

Leibniz, G. W.

1703 *Nouveaux Essais sur l'Entendement Humain* (Berlin).

Liaño Pacheco, J. M.

1971 *Sanctius El Brocense* (Madrid).

Linacer, T.

1524 *De emendata structura latini sermonis libri VI* (London).

Locke, J.

1690 *Essay Concerning Humane Understanding,* Book III: Of Words or Language in General (London).

Manthey, F.

1937 *Die Sprachphilosophie des hl. Thomas von Aquin und ihre Anwendung auf Probleme der Theologie* (Paderborn).

Marty, A.

1908 *Untersuchungen zur Grundlegung der allgemeinen Grammatik und Sprachphilosophie,* 1 (Halle).

Michelsen, C.

1837 *Historische Übersicht des Studiums der laeinischen Grammatik seit der Widerherstellung der Wissenschaften* (Hamburg).

Miklosich, F.

1883 *Subjektlose Sätze* (Vienna).

Moody, E. A.

1935 *The Logic of William of Ockham* (London).

Mullally, J. P.

1945 *The Summulae Logicales of Peter of Spain* (Notre Dame, Indiana).

Navarro Funes, A.

1929 "La teoría de la fromas gramaticales ségun el Brocense", *Boletin de la Universidad de Granada,* I.

O'Mahony, B. E.

1964 "A Mediaeval Semantic", *Laurentinum,* 5 (Rome).

Otto, A. (ed.)

1955 *Johannis Daci Opera = Corpus philosophorum danicorum medii aevi,* I, partes 1, 2 (Copenhagen).

1963 *Simonis Daci Opera* = *Corpus philosophorum danicorum medii aevi*, III (Copenhagen).

Peirce, C. S.
1931-34 *Collected Papers*, I-V (Cambridge, Mass.).

Pinborg, J.
1967 *Die Entwicklung der Sprachtheorie im Mittellalter* = *Beiträge zur Geschichte der Philosophie und Theologie des Mittelalters*, XLII, part 2.
1972 *Logik und Semantik im Mittelalter* (Stuttgart).
1973 "Some syntactical concepts in medieval grammar", *Classica et Mediaevalia Francisco Blatt septuagenario dedicata* (Copenhagen).

Pinborg, J. & H. Roos (ed.)
1969 *Boethii Daci Opera* = *Corpus philosophorum danicorum medii aevi*, VI, part 1 (Copenhagen).

de Rijk, L. M. (ed.)
1956 *Petrus Abaelardus: Dialectica* = *Wijsgerige teksten en studies*, I (Assen).
1971 "The Development of Suppositio naturalis in Mediaeval Logic", *Vivarium*, 9.

Robins, R. H.
1951 *Ancient and Mediaeval Grammatical Theory in Europe* (London).

Roos, H.
1961 *Martini de Dacia Opera* = *Corpus philosophorum danicorum medii aevi*, II (Copenhagen).

Rotta, P.
1909 *La filosofia del linguaggio nella patristica e nella scolastica* (Turin).

Sánchez Barrado, M.
1919 *La elipsis según el Brocense en relación con su sistema gramatical* (Segovia).

Sanctius Brocensis, Franciscus
1562 *Minerva: seu de causis linguae Latinae commentarius*, (Salamanca). See also 1587 (2nd) edition.

Sapir, E.

1921   *Language: An Introduction to the Study of Speech* (New York).

1930   *Totality* = *Linguistic Society of America, Language Monographs*, 6.

Saussure, Ferdinand de

1967   *Course de linguistique générale,* éd. critique par R. Engler (Weisbaden).

Sciopius, G.

1628   *Grammatica philosophica* (Milan).

Starobinski, J.

1971   *Les mots sous les mots. Les anagrammes de F. de Saussure* (Paris).

Stéfanini, J.

1973   "Les modistes et leur apport à la théorie de la grammaire et du signe linguistique", *Semiotica,* 8.

Stravinsky, I.

1947   *Poetics of Music* (New York).

Thurot, Ch.

1868   *Notices et extraits de divers manuscrits latins pour servir à l'histoire des doctrines grammaticales du Moyen Âge* (Paris).

Verburg, P. A.

1952   *Taal en functionaliteit: een historisch-kritische studie over de opvattingen aangaande de functies der taal* (Wageningen).

Wallerand, G.

1913   *Les Oeuvres de Siger de Courtrai* = *Les philosophes belges,* VIII (Louvain).

Webb, C. C. J. (ed.)

1929   *John of Salisbury, Metalogicon libri III* (Oxford).

Werner, K.

1877   "Die Sprachlogik des Johannes Duns Scotus", *Sitzungsberichte der Wiener Akademie der Wissenschaften,* 85, no. 3.

The Twentieth Century in European and American
*Linguistics: Movements and Continuity**

Dear friends! I was asked to speak at the present
Symposium devoted to the European background of American linguistics about the science of language in America
and in Europe in the twentieth century. Apparently this
topic was suggested because I witnessed the international
development of linguistic thought through the long period
of six decades—I followed this development first in the upper
classes of the Lazarev Institute of Oriental Languages, afterwards as a student of lingusitics and subsequently as a research fellow at Moscow University, then from 1920 in
Prague and in other West-European, especially Scandinavian,
centers of linguistic thought, and since the forties in America,
with frequent visits to other areas of intense linguistic
research.

As my eminent colleague Einar Haugen said in his
recent paper, "Half a Century of the Linguistic Society"
(Haugen, 1974), "each of us treasures his own memories."
Thus, may I refer to my first, though indirect, acquain-
tance with the LSA. In March of 1925, the pioneering
Czech scholar expert in both English and general linguistics,
Vilém Mathesius, together with his younger devoted colla-
borator in these two fields, Bohumil Trnka, invited Sergej

---

*With the permission of H. M. Hoenigswald, reprinted from
The European Background of American Linguistics, ed. by H. M.
Hoenigswald, Dordrecht, Foris, 1979, 162-173.

Karcevskij and me to a consultative meeting. Mathesius began by citing two events. The first of them was the tenth anniversary of the Moscow Linguistic Circle, which, let us add, was already dissolved at that time, yet whose creation in 1915 and whose vital activities were a durable stimulus in the Russian and international development of linguistics and poetics. On my arrival in Prague in 1920, Mathesius questioned me about the make-up and work of the Moscow Circle and said, "We will need such a team here also, but now it is still too early. We must wait for further advances." At the outset of our debates in 1925, he announced the most recent and impelling news—the formation of the Linguistic Society of America. Mathesius was one of those European linguists who followed with rapt attention and sympathy the impressive rise of American research in the science of language.

In October 1926, the Prague Linguistic Circle had its first meeting. It is wellknown that this Prague association, which, strange as it seems at first glance, has also been dissolved, gave in turn a powerful and lasting impetus to linguistic thought in Europe and elsewhere. From the beginning, there was a close connection between the Linguistic Society of America and the Prague Linguistic Circle. I don't know whether the young generation of scholars realizes how strong these relations were. N. S. Trubetzkoy's letters (Jakobson, 1975) reveal some new data on the manifold ties between American linguistics and the "école de Prague". At the end of 1931, Trubetzkoy, at the time immersed in the study of American Indian languages, emphasized that

> most of the American Indianists perfectly describe the sound systems, so that their outlines yield all the essentials for the phonological characteristics of any given language, including an explicit survey of the extant consonantal clusters with respect to the different positions within or between the morphemes.

Trubetzkoy had a very high opinion of the American linguist whom he called "my Leipzig comrade." This was Leonard Bloomfield, who in 1913 shared a bench with Trubetzkoy and Lucien Tesnière at Leskien's and Brugmann's lectures. Bloomfield (Hockett, 1970:247) praised "Trubetzkoy's excellent article on vowel systems" of 1929 and devoted his sagacious 1939 study on "Menomini Morphophonemics" (Hockett, 1970:351-62) to N. S. Trubetzkoy's memory.

The Prague Circle had very close ties with Edward Sapir. When we held the International Phonological Conference of 1930, Sapir, though unable to attend, kept up a lively correspondence with Trubetzkoy about his Prague assembly and the development of the inquiry into linguistic, especially phonological, structure. Almost nothing remains of this exchange. Those of Sapir's messages which had not been seized by the Gestapo were lost when the Viennese home of Trubetzkoy's widow was demolished by an air raid. In their turn, Trubetzkoy's letters perished when Sapir, at the end of his life, destroyed his entire epistolary archive. However, some quotations from Sapir's letters have survived in Trubetzkoy's correspondence, and others were cited by Trubetzkoy at our meetings. It is noteworthy that Sapir underscored the similarity of his and our approaches to the basic phonological problems.

These are not the only cases of the transoceanic propinquity between linguists of the American and of the Continental avantgarde. We may recollect and cite a remarkable document published in *Language* (vol. 18, 307-9). In August 1942 the Linguistic Society of America received a cable forwarded by the Soviet Scientists' Anti-Fascist Committee. This was a telegraphic letter of more than 4,000 words sent from Moscow and signed by a prominent Russian linguist, Grigorij Vinokur, the former secretary of the Moscow Linguistic Circle. In this cabled report Vinokur emphasized the particular affinity of the young Russian linguists, especially the Moscow phonologists, with the

pursuits and strivings of the LSA. He noted how profoundly
Sapir was valued by the linguists of the USSR. Apparently
the first foreign version of Sapir's *Language* was an excellent
Russian translation of this historic handbook by the Russian
linguist A. M. Suxotin, with interesting editorial notes about
the parallel paths in international linguistics.

In the light of all these and many other interconnections,
the question of purported hostility between American and
European linguists comes to naught. Any actual contact
puts an end to the belief that these were two separate and
impervious scientific worlds with two different, irrecon-
cilable ideologies. Sometimes we hear allegations that
American linguists repudiated their European colleagues,
particularly those who sought refuge in this country. I was
one of those whom the Second World War brought to the
Western hemisphere, and I must state that the true scholars,
the outstanding American linguists, met me with a fraternal
hospitality and with a sincere readiness for scientific cooperation. If there were signs of hostility and repudiation—and
they were indeed evident—they occurred solely on the side
of a few inveterate administrators and narrow-minded,
ingrained academic bureaucrats and operators, and I am
happy to acknowledge the unanimous moral support and
defence which came from such genuine men of science as
Charles Fries, Zellig Harris, Charles Morris, Kenneth Pike,
Meyer Schapiro, Morris Swadesh, Stith Thompson, Harry V.
Velten, Charles F. Voegelin, and many others.

One of the first American linguists whom I met on my
arrival in this country and who became a true friend of
mine was Leonard Bloomfield. Both orally and in writing,
he repeatedly expressed his aversion to any intolerance and
he struggled against "the blight of the odium theologicum"
and against "denouncing all persons who disagree" with
ones interest or opinion or "who merely choose to talk
about something else" (in 1946). The fact that one,
Bloomfield wrote, "disagrees with others, including me,

in methods and theories does not matter; it would be deadly to have one accepted doctrine" (in 1945). I recollect our cordial and vivid debates; Bloomfield wanted me to stay and work with him at Yale, and assured me that he would be happy to have someone with whom he could have real discussions. The great linguist severely repudiated any selfish and complacent parochialism.

From my first days in this country in June 1941 I experienced the deep truth in Bloomfield's later obituary judgment on Franz Boas: "His kindness and generosity knew no bounds" (Hockett, 1970:408). The fundamental role in American linguistics played by this German-born scholar, 28 years old at his arrival in the United States, was wisely appraised by Bloomfield: "The progress which has since been made in the recording and description of human speech has merely grown from the roots, stem, and mighty branches of Boas' life-work." As to the founder and skillful director of the *Handbook of American Indian Languages* himself, I recall his amiable, congenial house in Grantwood, New Jersey, where the host, with his keen sense of humor, used to say to his sister in my presence: "Jakobson *ist ein seltsamer Mann!* He thinks that I am an American linguist!"

Boas strongly believed in the international character of linguistics and of any genuine science and would never have agreed with an obstinate demand for a regional confinement of scientific theories and research. He professed that any analogy to a struggle for national interests in politics and economics was superficial and far-fetched. In the science of language there are no patented discoveries and no problems of intertribal or interpersonal competition, of regulations for imported and exported merchandise or dogma. The greater and closer the cooperation between linguists of the world, the vaster are the vistas of our science. Not only in the universe of languages, but also throughout the world of convergent development of bilateral diffusion.

One may add that isolationist tendencies in the scientific

life of the two hemispheres were mere transient and insignificant episodes and that the international role of American linguistics and, in particular, the transoceanic influence of the American achievements in the theory of language appear as early as the European models do in American linguistics.

During the second half of the past century it was Germany which witnessed the widest progress and expansion of comparative Indo-European studies. Yet the new and fecund ideas in general linguistics emerged outside the German scholarly world. Toward the end of the nineteenth century Karl Brugmann and August Leskien, the two leading German comparatists and proponents of the world-famed Leipzig school of neogrammarians, emphatically acknowledged the immense stimulation which the American linguist William Dwight Whitney gave to the European research in the history of languages by his original treatment of general principles and methods. At the same time, Ferdinand de Saussure (Jakobson, 1971:xxviii-xliii) stated that Whitney, without having himself written a single page of comparative philology, was the only one "to exert an influence on all study of comparative grammar," whereas in Germany linguistic science, which was allegedly born, developed, and cherished there by innumerable people, in Saussure's (as also in Whitney's) opinion never manifested "the slightest inclination to reach the degree of abstraction necessary to dominate what one is actually doing and why all that is done has its justification in the totality of sciences." Having returned at the end of his scholarly activities to the "theoretical view of language," Saussure repeatedly expressed his reverence for "the American Whitney, who never said a single word on these topics which was not right." Whitney's books of general linguistics were immediately translated into French, Italian, German, Dutch, and Swedish and had a far wider and stronger scientific influence in Europe than in his homeland.

For many years American students of language, absorbed in particulars, seemed to disregard Whitney's old warning to linguists in which he adjured them not to lose "sight of the grand truths and principles which underlie and give significance to their work, and the recognition of which ought to govern its course throughout" (1867). Leonard Bloomfield was actually the first American scholar who from his early steps in linguistic theory endeavored to revive Whitney's legacy in the study of language.

As a parallel to the earlier and deeper naturalization of Whitney's *Principles of Linguistic Science* in the Old World one may cite the reception of Saussure's *Cours de linguistique générale* in the New World. Although it opened a new epoch in the history of linguistics, the appearance of this posthumous publication found, at first, only a few linguists ready to accept the basic lessons of the late Genevan teacher. Originally most of the West-European specialists outside of his native Switzerland showed restraint toward Saussure's conception, and, strange to say, France was one of the countries particulary slow in assimilating his theory. One of the earliest open-minded appraisers and adherents of the *Cours* was an American scholar. Its first two editions were commented on by Bloomfield not only in the separate review of the *Cours* for the *Modern Language Journal* (1923-24; Hockett, 1970:106-109), but also in Bloomfield's critiques of Sapir's *Language* (1922; Hockett, 1970:91-94) and of Jespersen's *Philosophy of Grammar* (1927; Hockett 1970: 141-143), and in a few further texts, all of them made easily available by Charles F. Hockett in his magnificent anthology (1970).

According to the aforesaid review, the nineteenth century "took little or no interest in the general aspects of human speech," so that Saussure in his lectures on general linguistics "stood very nearly alone," and his posthumous work "has given us the theoretical basis for a science of human speech." In reviewing Sapir's *Language*, Bloomfield realizes that the question of influence or simply convergent

innovations is "of no scientific moment," but in passing he
notes the probability of Sapir's acquaintance with Saussure's
"book, which gives a theoretical foundation to the newer
trend of linguistic study." In particular, he is glad to see that
Sapir "deals with synchronic matters (to use de Saussure's
terminology) before he deals with diachronic, and gives to
the former as much space as to the latter."

Bloomfield subscribes not only to the sharp Saussurian
distinction between synchronic and diachronic linguistics, but
also to the further dichotomy advocated by the *Cours*, namely
a rigorous bifurcation of human speech (*langage*) into a perfectly uniform system (*langue*) and the actual speech-utterance
(*parole*). He professess full accord with the "fundamental
principles" of the *Cours* (Hockett, 1970:141-142; 107):

> For me, as for de Saussure . . . and, in a sense, for Sapir . . . ,
> all this, de Saussure's *la parole*, lies beyond the power of our
> science. . . . Our science can deal only with those features of
> language, de Saussure's *la langue*, which are common to all
> speakers of a community,—the phonemes, grammatical cate-
> gories, lexicon, and so on. . . . A grammatical or lexical state-
> ment is at bottom an abstraction.

But in Bloomfield's opinion, Saussure "proves intentionally
and in all due form: that psychology and phonetics do not
matter at all and are, in principle, irrelevant to the study of
language." The abstract features of Saussure's *la langue*
form a "system,—so rigid that without any adequate physio-
logic information and with psychology in a state of chaos,
we are," Bloomfield asserts, "nevertheless able to subject
it to scientific treatment."

According to Bloomfield's programmatic writings of
the twenties, the "newer trend" with its Saussurian theoretic
foundation "affects two critical points." First, and once
more he underscores this point in his paper of 1927 "On
Recent Work in General Linguistics" (Hockett, 1970:173-
190), Saussure's outline of the relation between "synchronic"

and "diachronic" science of language has given a "theoretical justification" to the present recognition of descriptive linguistics "beside historical, or rather as precedent to it" (1970:179). In this connection it is worth mentioning that even the striking divergence between the search for new ways in Saussure's synchronic linguistics and his stationary, nearly neo-grammarian attitude toward "linguistic history," was adopted by Bloomfield, who was disposed to believe that here one could hardly learn "anything of a fundamental sort that Leskien didn't know" (see Hockett, 1970:177-178 and 542).

Referring to the second critical point of the "modern trend" in linguistics, Bloomfield commends two restrictive definitions of its sole attainable goal: he cites the Saussurian argument for "*la langue,* the socially uniform language pattern" (Hockett, 1970:177) and Sapir's request for "an inquiry into the function and form of the arbitrary systems of symbolism that we term languages" (Hockett, 1970:92-93, 143).

When maintaining that this subject matter must be studied "in and for itself," Bloomfield literally reproduces the final words of the *Cours.* Strange as it seems, here he shows a closer adherence to the text of Saussure's published lectures that the lecturer himself. As has since been revealed, the final, italicized sentence of the *Cours*—"*la linguistique a pour unique et véritable objet la langue envisagée en elle-même et pour elle-même*"—though never uttered by the late teacher, was appended to the posthumous book by the editors-restorers of Saussure's lectures as "*l'idée fondamentale de ce cours.*" According to Saussure's genuine notes and lectures, language must not be viewed in isolation, but as a particular case among other systems of signs in the frame of a general science of signs which he terms *sémiologie.*

The close connection between Bloomfield's (and, one may add, Sapir's) initial steps in general linguistics and the European science of language, as well as Whitney's significance in the Old World, exemplify the continuous reciprocity between the linguists of the two hemispheres.

In his first approach to the "principle of the phoneme" Bloomfield pondered over the concepts developed by the school of Sweet, Passy, and Daniel Jones, and when we met, he cited his particular indebtedness to Henry Sweet's "classical treatise" on *The Practical Study of Languages* (1900).* From the very outset of his concern for phonemic problems, Bloomfield confronted the difference between the discreteness of phonemes and "the actual continuum of speech sound" and Saussure's opposition of *langue/parole* (Hockett, 1970:179) and he found "explicit formulations" in Baudouin de Courtenay's *Versuch einer Theorie der phonetischen Alternationen* of 1895 (Hockett, 1970:248). In this book he also got the fruitful concept and term *morpheme*, coined by Baudouin (Hockett, 1970:130). Upon the same label, likewise borrowed from Baudouin's terminology, French linguistic literature mistakenly imposed the meaning "affix".

There are certain classical works in the European linguistic tradition which have constantly attracted special attention and recognition in the American science of language. Thus, the two books which so captivated Noam Chomsky, one by Humboldt and one by Otto Jespersen, have more than once since their appearance evoked lively

---

*In *Cahiers Ferdinand de Saussure* 32 (1978, p. 69) Calvert Watkins published remarkable excerpts from Bloomfield's letter of December 23, 1919 to the specialist in Algonquin languages at the Smithsonian, Truman Michelson: "My models are Pāṇini and the kind of work done in I.-E. by my teacher, Professor Wackernagel. No preconceptions; find out which sound variations are distinctive (as to meaning), and then analyze morphology and syntax by putting together everything that is alike." Bloomfield asks whether Michelson has got hold of de Saussure's *Cours·de linguistique générale*: "I have not yet seen it, but Professor Wackernagel mentioned it in a letter and I have ordered it and am anxious to see it." The European and especially Swiss roots of Bloomfield's innovative search—Jakob Wackernagel and Ferdinand de Saussure—become still clearer.

and laudatory responses from American linguists: thus, in Sapir's estimation, "the new vistas of linguistic thought opened up by the work of Karl Wilhelm von Humboldt," and the latter's treatise *Über die Verschiedenheit des menschlichen Sprachbaues* compelled Bloomfield to admire "this great scholar's intuition"; as to Jespersen's masterpiece, Bernard Bloch in 1941 praised "the greatness of the *Philosophy of Grammar*," and Bloomfield's review of 1927 pointed out that by this book "English grammar will be forever enriched" (Hockett, 1970:143, 180).

The widespread myth of a sole and uniform American linguistic school and of its exclusive control throughout the country, at least during certain periods in the development of the science of language in the United States, is at variance with the actual situation. Neither the geographical nor the historical significance of one or another scientific trend can be based on the excessive number of students who, as Martin Joos neatly remarked (1957:v), "accept the current techniques without inquiring into what lay behind them." What really counts is the quality alone, both of theoretical and of empirical attainments.

In America, as well as in Europe, there has fortunately always been an imposing variety of approaches to the foundations, methods, and tasks of linguistics. In its initial output, the Linguistic Society of America displayed a remarkable diversity of views. Its first president Hermann Collitz of the Johns Hopkins University, in his inaugural address (December 28, 1924; Collitz 1925) on "The Scope and Aims of Linguistic Science", spoke about the rapidly improving conditions for a new advancement of "general or 'philosophical' grammar", which for a while "had to be satisfied with a back seat in linguistics." Collitz laid stress on the principal problems of general linguistics, one of which concerns "the relation between grammatical forms and mental categories." He referred in this connection to "an able study written by an American scholar, namely: *Grammar and Thinking*, by

Albert D. Sheffield" (New York: 1912; Hockett, 1970:34), a book, let us add, "heartily welcomed" in Bloomfield's review of 1912 as "a sensible volume on the larger aspects of language." The other concern of general linguistics was defined by Collitz as "uniformities and permanent or steadily recurring conditions in human speech generally." The latter item shortly thereafter became a subject of controversy in the gatherings and publications of the LSA: skeptics were disposed to deny the existence of general categories, as long as no linguist can know which of them, if any, exist in all languages of the world, whereas Sapir with an ever growing persistence worked on a series of preliminaries to his *Foundations of Language*, a wide-ranging program of universal grammar that he cherished till the end of his life.

The passage of the aforementioned inaugural address on the "mental categories" as correlates of external forms hinted at a question about to become for decades an enduring *casus belli* between two linguistic currents in America, where they have been nicknamed respectively "mentalism" and "mechanism" or "physicalism". With regard to the pivotal problems of general linguistics touched upon by Collitz, Bloomfield's prefatory article—"Why a Linguistic Society?"—for the first issue of the Society's journal *Language* (Hockett, 1970:109-112) adopted a conciliatory tone: "The science of language, dealing with the most basic and simplest of human social institutions, is a human (or mental or, as they used to say, moral) science. . . . It remains for linguists to determine what is widespread and what little is common to all human speech." Yet the two integral theoretical articles which made up the second issue of the same volume—Sapir's "Sound Patterns in Language" and "Linguistics and Psychology" by A. P. Weiss— brought to light a major scientific dissent. Sapir's epochal essay (1925), one of the most farsighted American contributions to the apprehension and advance of linguistic methodology, asserts from its first lines that no linguistic phenomena or processes, in particular neither sound patterns nor sound processes of speech (for instance "umlaut" or Grimm's law", so-called), can be properly understood in simple mechanical, sensorimotor terms. The dominant role was said to pertain to the "intuitive pattern alignment" proper to all speakers of a given language. According to the author's conclusion, the whole aim and spirit of the paper was to show that phonetic phenomena are not physical phenomena *per se* and to offer "a special illustration of the necessity of getting behind the sense data of any type of expression in order to grasp the intuitively felt and communicated forms which alone give significance to such expression."

Sapir's assaults against mechanistic approaches to language run counter to the radical behaviorism of the psychologist Albert Paul Weiss. The latter's article appeared in *Language* thanks to the sponsorship of Bloomfield, who taught with Weiss at Ohio State University, 1921-27, and who was increasingly influenced by his doctrine. In this paper of 1925 Weiss envisions a "compound multicellular type of organization" produced by language behavior, and he assigns to written language the rise of an even "more effective sensorimotor interchangeability between the living and the dead." Bloomfield's wide-scale outline of 1939, *Linguistic Aspects of Science,* with its numerous references to Weiss, picks up and develops this image: "Language bridges the gap between the individual nervous systems. . . . Much as single cells are combined in a many-celled animal, separate persons are combined in a speech community. . . . We may speak here, without metaphor, of a social organism."

What, however, most intimately fastens Bloomfield to the works of Weiss is the latter's demand that human behavior be discussed in physical terms only. "The relation between structural and behavior psychology," examined by Weiss in the *Psychological Review* (1917), rejects the structuralist's aim "to describe the structure of the mind or consciousness" and denies the possibility of cooperation between structuralism and behaviorism, so far as the fundamental conceptions underlying both methods and the theoretical implications of either method are subjected to a close scrutiny.

In conformity with these suggestions, any "mentalistic view" was proscribed by Bloomfield as a "prescientific approach to human things" or even a "primeval drug of animism" with its "teleologic and animistic verbiage": will, wish, desire, volition, emotion, sensation, perception, mind, idea, totality, consciousness, subconsciousness, belief, and the other "elusive spiritistic-teleologic words of our tribal speech." In the mentioned *Linguistic Aspects of Science* (Bloomfield, 1939:13) one chances to come across a paradoxically phrased confession: "It is the belief [!] of the present writer that the scientific description of the universe . . . requires none of the mentalistic terms." Bloomfield's presidential address to the Linguistic Society of America in 1935 prophesied that "within the next generations" the terminology of mentalism and animism "will be discarded, much as we have discarded Ptolemaic astronomy" (Hockett, 1970:322).

It is this drastic dissimilarity between the two leading spirits of the Linguistic Society in the very essence of their scientific creeds which found its plain expression in Sapir's oral remarks on "Bloomfield's sophomoric psychology" and in Bloomfield's sobriquet for Sapir, "medicine man" (Hockett, 1970:540). A diametrical opposition between both of them with regard to such matters as "the synthesis of linguistics with other sciences" was deliberately pointed to in Bloomfield's writings (Hockett, 1970:227, 249).

This difference between two methods of approach deepened with the years and greatly affected the course and fortunes of semantic research in American linguistics. On the one hand, the inquiry into the "communicative symbolism" of language in all its degrees and on all its levels, from the sound pattern through the grammatical and lexical concepts, to the "integrated meaning of continuous discourse," was becoming of still higher import in the work of Sapir, and with an avowed reference to his enlightening teaching, it was said in 1937 by Benjamin L. Whorf that "the very essence of linguistics is the quest for meaning" (1956:79). On the other hand, Bloomfield, though realizing perfectly that the treatment of speech-forms and even of their phonemic components "involves the consideration of meanings," admitted at the same time in his paper "Meaning" of 1943 that "the management of meanings is bound to give trouble" as long as one refuses to adopt "the popular (*mentalistic*) view" and to say "that speech forms reflect unobservable, non-physical events in the *minds* of speakers and hearers" (Hockett, 1970:401).

The difficulty in considering meaning while negating any "mental events" provoked repeated efforts by some younger language students to analyze linguistic structure without any reference to semantics, in contradistinction to Bloomfield's invocation of meaning as an inevitable criterion. Bloomfield himself was ready to deny not only the validity of such claims, but even the possibility of their existence (cp. Fries, 1954). Nonetheless, experiments in antisemantic linguistics became widespread toward the late forties. I was invited in the summer of 1945 to give a series of lectures at the University of Chicago. When I informed the University of my title for the planned cycle—"Meaning as the Pivotal Problem of Linguistics"—there came a benevolent warning from the faculty that the topic was risky.

It would be fallacious, however, to view the avoidance of semantic interpretation as a general and specific feature of the American linguistic methodology even for a brief stretch of time. This tentative ostracism was an interesting and fruitful trial accompanied by simultaneous and instructive criticism, and it has been superseded by an equally passionate and acclaimed striving for the promotion of semantic analysis first in vocabulary, then also in grammar.

Yet, finally, what bears a stamp of American origin is the semiotic science built by Charles Sanders Peirce from the 1860's throughout the late nineteenth and early twentieth centuries, a theory of signs to which, as was justly acknowledged (under Charles Morris' influence) by Bloomfield, "linguistics is the chief contributor," and which in turn has prepared the foundations for a true linguistic semantics. But in spite of this, Peirce's *semiotic* remained for many decades fatally unknown to the linguists of both the New and the Old World.

Now to sum up. In America the science of language produced several remarkable, prominent, internationally influential thinkers—to mention only some of those who are no longer with us, Whitney, Peirce, Boas, Sapir, Bloomfield, Whorf. What we observe at present, and what proves to be timely indeed, is an ever higher internationalization of linguistic science, without a ludicrous fear of foreign models and of "intellectual free trade."

One can still reproach American students and scholars, as well as those in diverse European countries, for a frequent inclination to confine the range of their scientific reading to books and papers issued in their native language and homeland and particulary to refer chiefly to local publications. In some cases this propensity results merely from an insufficient acquaintance with foreign languages, which is a debility widely spread among linguists. It is for this reason that important studies written in Russian and other Slavic languages have remained unknown, although some of them provide new and suggestive approaches.

One should finally mention the most negative phenomenon of American linguistic life. Bloomfield, who in 1912 had expressed " a modest hope . . . that the science of language may in time come to hold in America also its proper place among sciences" (Hockett, 1970:33), returned to this question in his notable survey, "Twenty-one Years of the Linguistic Society", shortly before the end of his scholarly activity. He was certainly right in concluding that "the external status of our science leaves much to be desired though there has been some improvement" (Hockett, 1970: 493). Now, however, this improvement is rapidly vanishing. Once again we observe that the blame does not lie with linguists, but with those bureaucrats who, under the pretext of scarcity and restraint, are prone to abolish or reduce departments and chairs of general linguistics, of comparative Indo-European studies, of Romance, Scandinavian, Slavic and other languages. In Sapir's pointed parlance, efforts are being made to establish and perpetuate the "very pallid status of linguistics in America," because this science seems to be hardly "convertible into cash value" (1925:4-150). Such antiscientific measures are most deplorable. In spite of the present crisis, America still remains more prosperous than most of the European countries, but even under their economic recession, none of them has dismantled its graduate schools and their linguistic programs. Nevertheless, permit me, in conclusion, once more to quote Leonard Bloomfield. The forecast made 45 years ago (December 30, 1929; Hockett, 1970:227) in his address before a joint meeting of the Linguistic Society of America and the Modern Languages Associations reads:

> I believe that in the near future—in the next few generations, let us say—linguistics will be one of the main sectors of scientific advance.

Do not all of us here share this belief?

References

Baudouin de Courtenay, Jan
1895 *Versuch einer Theorie phonetischer Alternationen.*

Bloch, Bernard
1941 Review of Jespersen, O., *Efficiency in Linguistic Change*, in *Language* 17:350-353.

Bloomfield, Leonard
1939 "Linguistic Aspects of Science", *International Encyclopedia of Unified Science* 1:4 (Chicago: University of Chicago Press).
[The remaining work is quoted by reference to Hockett, 1970.]

Collitz, Hermann
1925 "Scope and Aim of Linguistic Science", *Language* 1:14-16.

Fries, Charles C.
1954 "Meaning and Linguistic Analysis", *Language* 30:57-68.

Haugen, Einar
1974 "Half a Century of the Linguistic Society", *Language* 50:619-621.

Hockett, Charles F.
1970 *A Leonard Bloomfield Anthology* (Bloomington-London: Indiana University Press).

Jakobson, Roman
1971 "The World Response to Whitney's *Principles of Linguistic Science*", in Michael Silverstein (ed.), *Whitney on Language* (Cambridge [Mass.]-London: MIT Press).

1975 (ed.) *N. S. Trubetzkoy's Letters and Notes* (The Hague: Mouton).

Joos, Martin (ed.)
1957 *Readings in Linguistics* [I] (Washington: American Council of Learned Societies).

Sapir, Edward
1924 "The Grammarian and His Language", *American Mercury* 1:149-155.

Sweet, Henry
1899 *The Practical Study of Languages* (New York: Dent).

Weiss, Albert Paul
1917 "The Relation Between Structural and Behavior Psychology", *Psychological Review* 24:301-317.
1925 *A Theoretical Basis of Human Behavior* (Columbus: Adams).

Whitney, William Dwight
1867 *Language and the Study of Language. Twelve Lectures on the Principles of Linguistic Science* (New York: Scribner).

Whorf, Benjamin L.
1956 *Language, Thought and Reality* (Cambridge [Mass.] - London: MIT Press).

*Metalanguage as a Linguistic Problem**

Language must be investigated in all the variety of its functions. An outline of these functions demands a concise survey of the constitutive factors in any speech event, in any act of verbal communication. The ADDRESSER sends a MESSAGE to the ADDRESSEE. To be operative the message requires a CONTEXT referred to ("referent" in another, somewhat ambiguous nomenclature), seizable by the addressee, and either verbal or capable of being verbalized; a CODE fully, or at least partially, common to the addresser and addressee (or in other words, to the encoder and decoder of the message); and, finally, a CONTACT, a physical channel and psychological connection between the addresser and the addressee, enabling both of them to enter and stay in communication. The six different functions determined by these six factors may be schematized as follows:

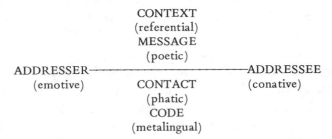

*The author dedicates this Presidential Address, delivered at the Annual Meeting of the Linguistic Society of America, December 27, 1956, to the memory of his true friend and the courageous champion of linguistic truth, Gyula Laziczius.

Although we distinguish six basic aspects of language, we could, however, hardly find verbal messages that would fulfill only one function. The diversity lies not in a monopoly of some one of these several functions but in their different hierarchical order. The verbal structure of a message depends primarily on the predominant function. But even though a set (*Einstellung*) toward the referent, an orientation toward the CONTEXT—briefly the so-called REFERENTIAL, "denotative", "cognitive" function—is the leading task of numerous messages, the accessory participation of the other functions in such messages must be taken into account by the observant linguist.

The so-called EMOTIVE or "expressive" function, focused on the ADDRESSER, aims a direct expression of the speaker's attitude toward what he is speaking about. It tends to produce an impression of a certain emotion whether true of feigned; therefore, the term "emotive", launched and advocated by Marty, has proved to be preferable to "emotional." The purely emotive stratum in language is presented by the interjections. They differ from the means of referential language both by their sound pattern (peculiar sound sequences or even sounds elsewhere unusual) and by their syntactic role (they are not components but equivalents of sentences). " '*Tut! Tut!*' said McGinty"; the complete utterance of Conan Doyle's character consists of two suction clicks. The emotive function, laid bare in the interjections, flavors to some extent all our utterances, on their phonic, grammatical, and lexical level. If we analyze language from the standpoint of the information it carries, we cannot restrict the notion of information to the cognitive, ideational aspect of language. A man, using expressive features to indicate his angry or ironic attitude, conveys ostensible information. The difference between [jɛs] "yes" and the emphatic prolongation of the vowel [jɛːs] is a conventional, coded linguistic feature like the difference between the short and long vowel in such Czech pairs as [vi] "you" and [viː]

"knows" but in the latter pair the differential information is phonemic and in the former emotive. As long as we are interested in phonemic invariants, the English [ɛ] and [ɛ:] appear to be mere variants of one and the same phoneme, but if we are concerned with emotive units, the relation between the invariant and variants is reversed: length and shortness are invariants implemented by variable phonemes.

Orientation toward the ADDRESSEE, the CONATIVE function, finds its purest grammatical expression in the vocative and imperative, which syntactically, morphologically, and often even phonemically deviate from other nominal and verbal categories. The imperative sentences cardinally differ from declarative sentences: the latter are and the former are not liable to a truth test. When in O'Neill's play *The Fountain* Nano, "(in a fierce tone of command)," says "Drink!"—the imperative cannot be challenged by the question, "Is it true or not?" which may be, however, perfectly well asked after such sentences as "one drank", "one will drink", "one would drink," or after such conversions of the imperative sentences into declarative sentences: "you will drink," "you have to drink," "I order you to drink." In contradistinction to the imperative sentences, the declarative sentences are convertible into interrogative sentences: "did one drink?", "will one drink?", "would one drink?", "do I order you to drink?"

The traditional model of language as elucidated in particular by Karl Bühler was confined to these three functions—emotive, conative, and referential—and to the three apexes of this model—the first person of the addresser, the second person of the addressee, and the "third person," properly—someone or something spoken of. Certain additional verbal functions can be easily inferred from this triadic model. Thus the magic, incantatory function is chiefly some kind of conversion of an absent or inanimate "third person" into an addressee of a conative message. "May this sty dry up, *tfu, tfu, tfu, tfu*" (Lithuanian spell).

"Water, queen river, daybreak! Send grief beyond the blue
sea, to the sea-bottom, like a grey stone never to rise from
the sea-bottom, may grief never come to burden the light
heart of God's servant, may grief be removed and sink
away." (North Russian incantation).   "Sun, stand thou
still upon Gibeon; and thou, Moon, in the valley of Aj-a-lon.
And the sun stood still, and the moon stayed . . ." (Josh.
10.12).   We observe, however, three further constitutive
factors of verbal communication and three corresponding
functions of language.

There are messages primarily serving to establish, to
prolong, or to discontinue communication, to check whether
the channel works ("Hello, do you hear me?"), to attract
the attention of the interlocutor or to confirm his continued
attention ("Are you listening?" or in Shakespearean diction,
"Lend me your ears!"—and on the other end of the wire
"Um-hum!"). This set for CONTACT, or in B. Malinowski's
terms PHATIC function, may be displayed by a profuse
exchange of ritualized formulas, by entire dialogues with the
mere purport of prolonging communication. Dorothy Parker
caught eloquent examples: " 'Well!' she said. 'Well, here
we are,' he said. 'Here we are,' she said, 'Aren't we?' 'I should
say we were,' he said, 'Eeyop! Here we are.' 'Well!' she
said. 'Well!' he said, 'well.' "   The endeavor to start and
sustain communication is typical of talking birds; thus the
phatic function of language is the only one they share with
human beings when conversing with them. It is also the first
verbal function acquired by infants; they are prone to communication before being able to send or receive informative
communication.

The set (*Einstellung*) toward the MESSAGE as such,
focus on the message for its own sake, is the POETIC function of language. This function cannot be productively
studied out of touch with the general problems of language,
and, on the other hand, the scrutiny of language requires
a thorough consideration of its poetic function. Any attempt

to reduce the sphere of poetic function to poetry or to confine poetry to poetic function would be a delusive over-simplification. Poetic function is not the sole function of verbal art but only its dominant, determining function, whereas in other verbal activities it acts as a subsidiary, accessory constituent. This function, by promoting the palpability of signs, deepens the fundamental dichotomy of signs and objects. Hence, when dealing with poetic function, linguistics cannot limit itself to the field of poetry.

"Why do you always say *Joan and Margery*, yet never *Margery and Joan?* Do you prefer Joan to her twin sister?" "Not at all, it just sounds smoother." In a sequence of two coordinate names, as far as no rank problems interfere, the precedence of the shorter name suits the speaker, unaccountably for him, as a well-ordered shape of the message.

A girl used to talk about "the horrible Harry." "Why horrible?" "Because I hate him." But why not *dreadful, terrible, frightful, disgusting?*" "I don't know why, but *horrible* fits him better." Without realizing it, she clung to the poetic device of paronomasia.

Two alliterative clusters must have favored the coalescence of "French fries" into a habitual phrase-word.

The political slogan "I like Ike" [ay layk ayk], succinctly structured, consists of three monosyllables and counts three dipthongs [ay], each of them symmetrically followed by one consonantal phoneme [. . l . . k . . k]. The setup of the three words shows a variation: no consonantal phonemes in the first word, two around the dipthong in the second, and one final consonant in the third. Both cola of the trisyllabic formula "I like/Ike" rhyme with each other, and the second of the two rhyming words is fully included in the first one (echo rhyme), [layk] — [ayk], a paronomastic image of a feeling which totally envelops its object. Both cola alliterate with each other, and the first of the two alliterating words is included in the second: [ay] — [ayk], a paronomastic image of the loving subject enveloped by the beloved object. The secondary, poetic function of this electional catchphrase reinforces its impressiveness and efficacy.

A discrimination clearly anticipated by the Ancient Greek and Indic tradition and pushed forward by the medieval treatise *de suppositionibus* has been advocated in modern logic as a need to distinguish between two levels of language, namely the "object language" speaking of items extraneous to language as such, and on the other hand a language in which we speak about the verbal code itself. The latter aspect of language is called "metalanguage", a loan-translation of the Polish term launched in the 1930s by Alfred Tarski. On these two different levels of language the same verbal stock may be used; thus we may speak in English (as metalanguage) about English (as object language) and interpret English words and sentences by means of English synonyms and circumlocutions. Jeremy Bentham respectively delineates "expositions by translation and by paraphrasis." Like Moliere's Jourdain, who used prose without knowing that it was prose, we practice metalanguage without realizing the metalingual character of our statements. Far from being confined to the sphere of science, metalingual operations prove to be an integral part of our verbal activities. Whenever the addresser and/or the addressee need to check up whether they use the same code, speech is focused upon the CODE and thus performs a METALINGUAL (or glossing) function. "I don't follow you—what do you mean?" asks the addressee, or in Shakespearean diction, "What is't thou say'st?" And the addresser in anticipation of such recapturing questions inquires: "Do you know what I mean?" Then, by replacing the questionable sign with another sign or a whole group of signs from the same or another linguistic code, the encoder of the message seeks to make it more accessible to the decoder.

—I eagerly brought out: "But not to the degree to contaminate." "To contaminate?"—my big word left her at a loss. I explained it. "To corrupt." She stared, taking my meaning in (Henry James, *The Turn of the Screw*).

—It done her in . . .—What does doing her in mean?—Oh, that's the new small talk. To do a person in means to kill them.—You surely don't believe that your aunt was killed? —Do I no! (G. B. Shaw, *Pygmalion*).

Or imagine such an exasperating dialogue.—"The sophomore was plucked." "But what is *plucked*?" "*Plucked* means the same as flunked." "To be *flunked* is *to fail in an exam*." "And what is *sophomore*?" persists the interrogator innocent of school vocabulary. "A *sophomore* is (or means) a *second-year student*."

Such equational propositions ordinarily used by interlocutors nullify the idea of verbal meanings as "subjective intangibles" and become particularly conspicuous in cases of their reversibility: "A second-year student is (called) a sophomore"; "A gander is an adult male goose", but also conversely "An adult male goose is a gander." The former proposition is an example of C. S. Peirce's thesis that any sign translates itself into other signs in which it is more fully developed, whereas the reverse translation from a more explicit to a terser way of expression is exemplified by the latter proposition.

Signs are viewed by Peirce as equivalent "when either might have been an interpretant of the other." It must be emphasized again and again that the basic, immediate, "selective" interpretant of any sign is "all that is explicit in the sign itself apart from its context and circumstance of utterance" or in more unified terms: apart from its context either verbal or only verbalizable but not actually verbalized. Peirce's semiotic doctrine is the only sound basis for a strictly linguistic semantics. One can't help but agree with his view of meaning as translatability of a sign into a network of other signs and with his reiterated emphasis on the inherence of a "general meaning" in any "genuine symbol", as well as with the sequel of the quoted assertion: A symbol "cannot indicate any particular thing: it denotes a kind of thing. Not only that, but it is itself a kind and not a single thing" (*Collected Papers,* 2.301). The contextual meanings which particularize, specify, or even modify such a general meaning are dealt with in Peirce's speculative grammar as secondary, "environmental" interpretants.

In spite of some students' objections, it is clear that the "selective interpretant" of a proper name, too, necessarily has a more general character than any single "environmental interpretant". The context indicates whether we speak about Napolean in his infancy, the hero of Austerlitz, the loser at Waterloo, the prisoner on his deathbed, or a hero in posthumous tradition, whereas his name in its general meaning encompasses all these stages of his life and fate. Like the metabolic insect in the sequence *caterpillar-pupa-butterfly,* a person may even acquire different names for consecutive temporal segments, "momentary objects" in W. V. Quine's terminology. Married name is substituted for maiden name, monastic for secular. Of course, each of these named stages could be further segmented.

Metalingual operations with words or syntactic constructions permit us to overcome Leonard Bloomfield's forebodings in his endeavors to incorporate meaning into the science of language. Thus, for instance, the alleged difficulty of describing meanings in these cases "of words like *but, if, because*" has been disproved by the treatment of conjunctions in symbolic logic, and such anthropological studies as *Les structures élémentaires de la parenté* by Claude Lévi-Strauss have proved the groundlessness of assumptions that the various terminologies of kinship "are extremely hard to analyze." Yet on the whole Bloomfield's justified view of "one of the meanings as *normal* (or *central*) and the others as *marginal (metaphoric* or *transferred*)*"* requires a consistent application in semantic analysis: "The central meaning is favored in the sense that we understand a form (that is, respond to it) in the central meaning unless some feature of the practical situation forces us to look to a transferred meaning." Such is the contextual metaphoric use of *gander* or *goose* in application to a person who resembles the bird in stupidity. The same word in the contextual meaning "look, glance" is a metonymic transfer from the goose to its outstretched neck and goggling eyes in a metaphoric application to a human being. *Goose* is a designation of a bird species with no reference to sex but in contexts opposing *goose* to *gander*, the narrowed meaning of the former vocable is confined to the females. The opposite transfer, Bloomfield's widened meanings, may be exemplified by the use of the phrase-word *morning-star* to designate the planet Venus without reference to the time of its appearance. The literal, untransferred meaning of the two phrase-words, *morning-star* and *evening-star* becomes apparent, for example, if during an evening stroll, by a casual slip of the tongue one would bring to the attention of his perplexed partner the bright emergence of the *morning-star*. In contradistinction to the indiscriminate label *Venus*, the two phrase words, discussed by G. Frege, are actually suitable to define and to *name* two different spatio-temporal phases of one planet in relation to another one.

A relational divergence underlies the semantic variance of near-synonyms. Thus, the adjectives *half-full* and *half-empty* refer to quantitatively the same status of the bottle, but the former attribute used by the anecdotal optimist and the latter one substituted by the pessimist betray two opposite frames of reference, the full and the empty bottle. Two slightly deviant frames of reference separate the anticipatory *twenty minutes to six* from the retrospective *five forty*.

The constant use of metalingual commutations within the actual corpus of any given language offers a groundwork for a description and analysis of lexical and grammatical meanings which complies even with the platform of those inquirers who still believe that "the determining

criteria will always have to be stated in distributional terms."
Let us cite such pairs of reversible propositions as "hermaphrodites are individuals combining the sex organs of both
male and female"—"individuals combining the sex organs
of both male and female are hermaphrodites", or such
pairs as "centaurs are individuals combining the human
head, arms, and trunk with the body and legs of a horse"—
"individuals combining the human head, arms, and trunk
with the body and legs of a horse are centaurs." In those
two pairs we are faced with metalingual statements which
impart information about the meaning assigned to the
word *hermaphrodite* and *centaur* in the English vocabulary,
but which say nothing about the ontological status of the
individuals named. We apperceive the semantic difference
between the nouns *ambrosia* and *nectar* or between *centaur*
and *sphinx* and we can, for instance, transmute the two
latter words into pictures or sculptures, despite the absence
of such kinds of individuals in our experience. The words
in question may even be used not only in a literal but also
in a deliberately figurative meaning: *ambrosia* as a food
which gives us divine delight; *sphinx* as a designation of an
enigmatic person.

Statements of existence or nonexistence in regard to
such fictional entities gave rise to lengthy philosophical
controversies, but from a linguistic point of view the verb
of existence remains elliptic as far as it is not accompanied
by a locative modifier: "unicorns do not exist in the fauna
of the globe"; "unicorns exist in Greco-Roman and Chinese
mythology", "in the tapestry tradition", "in poetry", "in
our dreams", etc. Here we observe the linguistic relevance
of the notion *Universe of Discourse,* introduced by A. De
Morgan and applied by Peirce: "At one time it may be
the physical universe, at another it may be the imaginary
'world' of some play or novel, at another a range of possibilities." Whether directly referred to or merely implied
in an exchange of messages between interlocutors, this

notion remains the relevant one for a linguistic approach to semantics.

When the universe of discourse prompts a technological nomenclature, *dog* is sensed as a name of various gripping and holding tools, while *horse* designates various supportive devices. In Russian *kon'ki* "little horses" became a name of skates. Two contiguous stanzas of Pushkin's *Eugene Onegin* (Fourth Chapter, XLII-XLIII) depict the country in early winter, and the gaiety of the little peasant boys cutting the new ice with their skates (little horses) is confronted with the tedious time of the landlord whose helpless saddle horse stumbles over the ice. The poet's clearcut contrastive parallelism of *kon'ki* and *kon'* "horse" gets lost in translation into languages without the equine image of the skates. The conversion of *kon'ki* from animals into inanimate tools of locomotion, with a corresponding change in the declensional paradigm, has been effected under a metalingual control.

Metalanguage is the vital factor of any verbal development. The interpretation of one linguistic sign through other, in some respect homogeneous, signs of the same language, is a metalingual operation which plays an essential role in child language learning. Observations made during recent decades, in particular by the Russian inquirers A. N. Gvozdev and K. I. Čukovskij, have disclosed what an enormous place talk about language occupies in the verbal behavior of preschool children, who are prone to compare new acquisitions with earlier ones and their own way of speaking with the diverse forms of speech used by the older and younger people surrounding them; the makeup and choice of words and sentences, their sound, shape and meaning, synonymy and homonymy are vividly discussed. A constant recourse to metalanguage is indispensable both for a creative assimilation of the mother tongue and for its final mastery.

Metalanguage is deficient in aphasics with a similarity disorder, labeled "sensory impairment"; despite instructions, they cannot respond to the stimulus word of the examiner with an equivalent word or expression and lack the capacity for building equational propositions.   Any aptitude for translation, either intralingual or interlingual, is lost by these patients.

The buildup of the first language implies an aptitude for metalingual operations, and no familiarization with further languages is possible without the development of this aptitude; the breakdown of metalanguage plays a substantial part in verbal disturbances.   Finally, the urgent task which faces the science of language, a systematic analysis of lexical and grammatical meanings, must begin by approaching metalanguage as an innermost linguistic problem.

We realize ever more clearly that any verbal message in the selection and combination of its constituents involves a recourse to the given code and that a set of latent metalingual operations underlies this perpetual framework.

Après tout, c'est ainsi que nous communiquons, par des phrases, meme tronquées, embryonnaires, incomplètes, mais toujours par des phrases. C'est ici, dans notre analyse, un point crucial.

—Émile Benveniste
3 septembre 1966

On Aphasic Disorders from a Linguistic Angle*

Over three decades ago, in 1941, when I was about to publish my first study dealing with aphasia, *Child Language, Aphasia, and Phonological Universals* (Jakobson, 1968), I was surprised at the extent to which linguists neglected questions concerning children's buildup and pathological disruptions of language. In particular, the field of aphasia was usually disregarded. There were, however, a few neurologists and psychologists who insisted on the important role that linguistics can play in this domain. They realized that aphasia is first and foremost a disintegration of *language*, and as linguists deal with language, it is linguists who have to tell us what the exact nature of these diverse disintegrations is. Such were the questions raised, for instance, by A. Pick (1920), A. Gelb (1924), K. Goldstein (1932), and M. Isserlin (1922). But among linguists themselves there reigned a total indifference to problems of aphasia. Of course, as always, one can find exceptions.

Thus from the early 1870's, one of the greatest precursors of modern linguistics, Jan Baudouin de Courtenay, consistently observed and investigated cases of aphasia and in

---

*C'est à Émile Benveniste qui fut l'un des premiers à soutenir l'importance des études strictement linguistiques sur les syndromes de l'aphasie que je tiens à dédier en hommage d'admiration et affection cette étude basée sur mes rapports au Troisième Symposion International d'Aphasiologie à Oaxtepec, Mexique, novembre 1971, et au Congreso Peruano de Patologia del Lenguaje à Lima, Peru, octobre 1973.

1885 devoted to one of them a detailed Polish monograph, *From the Pathology and Embryology of Language* (Baudouin de Courtenay, 1885-1886), which was supposed to be followed by further papers. This study combines a rich and careful collection of data with an emphasis on the vital necessity of inquiring into child language and aphasia for linguistic theory and phonetics. Prospects for finding general laws based on the comparison of aphasic syndromes with systems of ethnic languages were anticipated. A few decades later, Ferdinand de Saussure, in sketching a review of A. Sechehaye's *Programme et méthodes de la linguistique théorique* (1908), underscored the relevance of Broca's discoveries and of pathological observations on the diverse forms of aphasia, which have especial interest for the relations between psychology and grammar: "Je rappelle par exemple les cas d'aphasie où la catégorie des substantifs tout entière manque, alors que les autres catégories établies du point de vue de la logique restent à la disposition du sujet" (Godel, 1957).

These significant calls remained, however, as most of Baudouin's and Saussure's exhortations, without any immediate response. But at present, beginning with the forties and early fifties, one observes a substantial change. It becomes ever clearer "à quel point l'approche linguistique peut renouveler l'étude de l'aphasie," as has been pointed out in H. Hécaen's and R. Angelerque's *Pathologie du langage* (1965): "Il faut, en effet, que toutes les utilisations du langage libre et conditionné soient analysées à tous les niveaux du système linguistique."

The question of levels is relevant indeed. Too often, attempts to treat the linguistic aspect of aphasia suffer from inadequate delimitation of the linguistic levels. One could even say that today the most important task in linguistics is to learn how to delimit the levels. The various levels of language are autonomous. Autonomy doesn't mean isolationism; all levels are interrelated. Autonomy does not exclude integration, and even more—autonomy and integration are closely linked phenomena. But in all linguistic questions and especially in the case of aphasia, it is important to approach language and its disruption in the framework of a given level, while remembering at the same time that any level is what the Germans call *das Teilganze* and that the totality and the interralation between the different parts of the totality have to be taken into account. Here very often linguists commit a dangerous error, namely, they approach certain levels of language with an attitude of heteronomy (colonialism), rather than of autonomy. They treat one level only from the point of view of another level. In particular, when dealing with aphasia, we must immediately recognize that the phonological level, though of course it is not isolated, maintains its autonomy and cannot be viewed as a simple colony of the grammatical level.

One must take into account the interplay of *variety* and *unity*. As Hécaen states, "l'aphasie est en même temps une et multiple." The mutiple forms of linguistic disintegration must be distinguished, and it would be erroneous to study this multiplicity from a merely quantitative point of view, as if we were merely dealing with different degrees of disintegration, whereas in fact we face a significant qualitative diversity as well.

Furthermore, when we discuss those forms of aphasia in which disruption of the sound-pattern of language is a relevant factor, we must remember that for contemporary linguistics there is no such field as sounds for themselves only. For the speaker and listener speech sounds necessarily act as carriers of meaning. Sound and meaning are, both for language and for linguistics, an indissoluble duality. Neither of these factors can be considered as a simple colony of the other: the duality of sound and meaning must be studied both from the angle of sound and from that of meaning. The degree to which speech sounds are a completely peculiar phenomenon among auditory events was made clear by the remarkable experiments conducted in diverse countries during the last decade: these investigations have proved the privileged position of the right ear, connected with the left hemisphere, in perceiving speech sounds. Is it not a remarkable fact that the right ear is a better receptor of speech components, in contradistinction to the superiority of the left ear for all non-verbal sounds, whether musical tones or noises? This shows that from the beginning speech sounds appear as a particular category to which the human brain reacts in a specific way, and this peculiarity is due precisely to the fact that speech sounds fulfill a quite distinct and multifarious role: in different ways they function as carriers of meaning.

When we study the diverse linguistic syndromes of aphasia, we must pay consistent attention to the hierarchy of linguistic constituents and their combinations. We begin with the ultimate discrete units of language, "distinctive features", or *mérismes,* as Benveniste proposed to call them (Benveniste, 1966:121). The fundamental role played by the identification and discrimination of these linguistic quanta in speech perception and in its aphasic disruptions has been exhaustively investigated and convincingly shown by Sheila Blumstein who combines a thorough training in linguistics and neurology (1973, *cf.* Goodglass & Blumstein, 1973). The French equivalent of "distinctive feature" is *trait distinctif* or, in Saussure's occasional nomenclature, *élement differentiel,* whereas the term *trait pertinent,* sometimes used by French linguists, is misleading, because any constituent of language proves to be pertinent in some respect and the notions of distinctiveness and pertinence do not coincide.

The bundle of concurrent distinctive features is labeled "phoneme", according to the French term *phonème,* introduced in the 1870's and gradually redefined. It is an important and useful concept on the condition that one realizes its derived, from the viewpoint of linguistic structure, secondary character in relation to its components, the distinctive features. The exaggerated attempts to abolish the concept of phoneme are as equally unfounded as the opposite retrograde efforts to minimalize or even to discard the concept of distinctive features in favor of phonemes. In the summary of her monograph, S. Blumstein points out that "the notion *distinctive feature* has provided a principled explanation for the frequency of the different types of substitution errors made by aphasics" and that "moreover, the strategies for speech production demonstrated by aphasic patients suggested that the binary values ascribed to features in phonological theory may be an intrinsic part of the phonological system of the speaker." The basic structural principle of these values, namely the opposition of marked and unmarked entities, proves to be "an essential aspect of phonoological analyses, because "the notion markedness characterised the direction of substitution and simplification errors made by aphasics."

The smallest unit that carries its own meaning is the "morpheme", a concept and term introduced by Baudouin de Courtenay. Unfortunately, French linguistic terminology, according to Meillet's testimony, adopted and utilized this term in a narrowed sense in order to translate Brugmann's German label *formant*, appliable to affixes but not to the root, and certain annoying vacillations resulted in French grammatical nomenclature.

About the highest morphological unit, the "word" (*mot*), one can repeat what was said in reference to the phoneme: it is a substantial concept that can be neither discarded nor considered as the ultimate grammatical unit instead of the morpheme.

The usual English hierarchy of syntactic structures— "phrase", "clause", "sentence"—proves useful in the analysis of spontaneous and conditioned aphasic speech. The French terminology is less stable. Perhaps Lucien Tesnière's *noued* (1959) for the English "phrase" and the traditional French names *proposition* and *phrase* for "clause" and "sentence" would be appropriate.

When I worked on a linguistic interpretation of aphasic data and then ventured to systematise the analysed material in the light of strictly linguistic criteria, step by step I observed salient correspondences between the linguistic types of aphasia and the topographic syndromes discovered by experts in studies of the cortex, especially by A. R. Luria (1964, 1966), and I outlined these manifest parallels in my papers of 1963 and 1966 (see Jakobson, 1971). I prefer, however, to avoid making equations without having submitted them to a systematic interdisciplinary control, and my own work remains concentrated upon the verbal aspect of aphasia in its manifold ramifications. But I feel deeply impressed and inspired when reading the recent synthetic study of A. R. Luria, the great inquirer into cerebral mechanisms and their lesions as factors of the different kinds of aphasic disorders (Luria, 1973a). When this creator of neurolinguistics (*cf.* Luria, 1973), in developing his unwearying research of speech disturbances, expresses his "full agreement with the basic concepts proposed" in my linguistic attempts to detect and classify the linquistic syndromes of aphasia and offers further, decisive references to the "physiological mechanisms underlying these impairments", the cardinal conclusion one may draw is the necessity of an ever closer cooperation between linguists and neurologists, a joint and consistent scrutiny which promises to open a deeper insight into the still unexplored mysteries both of the brain and of language.

We must not only correlate by also consistently discriminate two basically different phenomena, emission and reception. To use the terms of Charles Sanders Peirce, there are two distinct *dramatis personae,* in the "sayer" and the "sayee". Their attitudes toward code and message are quite different, and in particular, ambiguity, especially homonymy, is a problem faced only by the "sayee". Without the help of the context or situation, upon hearing "sun", he does not know whether "sun" or "son" is meant, whereas the "sayer" is innerly free of the "sayee's" probabilistic attitude, although he obviously may take account of the sayee's attitude and prevent some of the latter's homonymic handicaps. To illustrate the difference between the pattern of the sayer and that of the sayee, may I confess that although I succeed in following a clear-cut Italian speech, I am almost unable to produce a single sentence in this language. Thus, in respect to Italian I cannot act as an addresser but only as an addressee, either silent or replying in a different language. In studying aphasia, we must keep in mind the possibility of a radical separation between these two *competences* and the quite usual privileged position of reception over emission. Such is the status of infants who have learned to understand the language of adults but are themselves unable to say anything. The capability of decoding can arise before and, in the case of aphasics, separately from the ability to encode.

I prefer to delay the discussion on my phonological experience in aphasia and on the new aspects of the linguistic inquiry into the troubles and disruptions of the sound pattern, despite the fascinating outlook which these questions open at present to phonology. If in going over to a higher, properly grammatical level of aphasia and pursuing the principle of explicative adequacy, we confine ourselves to its rigorously linguistic analysis of verbal impairments, we are led to obtain a clear and simple picture of them. Yet to grasp the linguistic syndrome of a given type of aphasia, we must follow several guidelines.

First, a zoologist would not begin to study the difference between plants and animals by examining such transitional species as sponges and corals. One would hardly begin to study sexes by concentrating attention on hermaphrodites. Of course there are many hybrid, complex, mixed cases of aphasia, but we are unaware of the existence of clearly polarized types, and these strictly distinct, so to say, "pure" cases, as neurologists call them, should underlie our study and classification of aphasics and subsequently guide us also in our inquiry into borderline occurrences, whatever their frequency may be.

Secondly, the significant difference between spontaneous and conditioned speech, a fact well known to linguists, must be carefully applied to the study of aphasia as well. In addition to the answers a patient makes to the doctor's questions, we have to observe the aphasic's totally spontaneous speech, especially in his familiar surroundings, and compare these two structurally distinct types of utterances. When approaching the question of required reproduction and repetition, one must remember that these processes occupy a very particular place in our verbal behavior. At the London Symposium on Disorders of Language held in 1963 at the Ciba Foundation, the linguist A. S. C. Ross spoke about the need for corpora of aphasic texts, published or mimeographed, with utterances emitted in various types of discourse and with different interlocutors (1964). Such material is absolutely indispensable for obtaining a linguistic description and classification of aphasic syndromes. Reliable linguistic conclusions cannot be made on the basis of a mere collection of patients' answers to the doctor's questions, posed, moreover, under quite artificial conditions of medical interrogation.

From a linguistic point of view perhaps the clearest forms of aphasia were obtained in cases of outright agrammatism. We posses the remarkable insights into such cases by experts in aphasia like A. Pick (1913),Isserlin (1922),and E. Salomon (1914) in the past, or at present, H. Hécaen (1972; *cf.* Cohen & Hécaen, 1965) and H. Goodglass (1968; *cf.* Goodglass & Hunt, 1958) and their linguistic collaborators. It was Goodglass who found a consistent and revealing order in the aphasics' treatment of an English inflectional suffix, a triple homonym carrying three completely different grammatical functions, namely the suffix /-z/, with its two positional variants /-iz/ and /-s/. This suffix with the same positional variants is used in the plural of nouns, e. g. "dreams", in the possessive fore, e. g. "John's dream", and in the third person of present, e. g. "John dreams", while the last form to survive is the nominal plural, "dreams" (Goodglass & Berko, 1968). In children's acquisition of language we find just the opposite order, a mirror image: the plural "dreams" is the first form to appear, the subsequent acquisition is "John's dream", followed finally, by the third person "John dreams" (Benveniste, 1966). The actual explanation lies in the hierarchy of levels: the plural form, "dreams", is one *word*, which implies no syntactic sequences, whereas the possessive, "John's", implies the *phrase* level, where "John's" is a modifier dependent on some headword like "dream", and finally, the third person, "dreams", requires a *clause* with a subject and predicate.

It is completely clear that more complex syntactic structures are the first to be discarded, and the first to be lost in the cases of agrammatism is the relation between the subject and predicate. Children begin with one-word phrases (holophrases), then they reach the actual phrase level, "little boy", "black cat", "John's hat", etc., and the latest to emerge is the construction of subject and predicate. The acquisition of such constructions is, as a matter of fact, a verbal and mental revolution. Only at this stage does a real language, independent of the *hic et nunc,* appear. Scholars used to speak about a "psychological predicate" in the case of a child who sees a cat and says "cat". This holophrase was interpreted as a predicate appended to the animal which is seen by the infant. But only when the child gains the ability to express both the subject and the predicate in their interrelation, only at this dichotomous stage, does language come into its own. Observers of children's language in various countries have witnessed diverse variants of one and the same event. A boy of some two-three years comes to his father and says "dog meow" (or "meows"), and the parent corrects him by saying, "No, the cat meows and the dog barks." The child gets angry and cries. If however, the father is ready to take part in the game and say, "Yes, the dog meows, and Peter meows, and Mommy also meows, but the cat and uncle bark," the child is usually happy. However, it may happen that the little speaker gets angry precisely at such a responsive father, because he believes that talking about meowing dogs is his childish privilege, which adults have no right to assume. The story reflects an important linguistic fact: in learning his mother tongue, the child realizes that he has the right to impose different predicates on the same subject, "dog" ("the dog . . . runs, sleeps, eats, barks") as well as he may combine different subjects ("dog, cat, Peter, Mommy") with one and the same predicate (e.g. "runs"). Then why not extend this freedom to assign new predicates and say "the dog meows"? The misuses of freedom is a typical side-effect of the child's verbal and mental liberation from the given situation. As long as he merely says "runs", or "cat", or "dog", he is totally dependent on the present temporal and spatial environment, but with the appearance of subject-predicate clauses, he suddenly can speak of things distant in time or space, events belonging to the remote past or to the future, and furthermore he can build entire fictions. It is this ability that gets lost in cases of outright agrammatical aphasia.

Observations about imperatives in the acquisition and dissolution of language are most instructive. Imperative structures do not imply the existence of the clause pattern with its interplay of subject and predicate. Surmises that the imperative is a mere transform of a declarative verbal structure are deprived of any foundation. The imperative is the most elementary verbal form. For this very reason the imperative, which appears in the earliest stratum of children's language, is the most resistent in agrammatical aphasia, and the frequent tendency in inflectional languages to confine the imperative form to the bare root is in turn a convincing illustration of its primitive essence.

The absence of personal pronouns, which surprised investigators of agrammatism, is parallel to the disappearance of relational spatio-temporal markers. These phenomena enter into the category of "shifters", viz. those grammatical classes which imply in their general meaning a reference to that message where they appear (cf. Jakobson, 1971a). These duplex, overlapping classes are typical marked super-structures in the grammatical system, and this fact explains their late emergence in children's language and their early disappearance in classical cases of agrammatical aphasia.

When we approach the type of disturbance that was recently outlined by J. Dubois, H. Hécaen et. al. (1970; cf. Beyn, 1957), the so-called "sensory" aphasia, and compare it with agrammatism, the linguistic polarity between these two types of aphasia becomes particularly obvious. Point by point one could show a pure, genuine opposition between the two syndromes. The central point of divergence lies in the fact that in the so-called sensory aphasia the nuclear elements of the grammatical structure, nouns, tend to disappear, whereas for agrammatical patients it is precisely nouns which form the basic stock of their vocabulary. Sensory aphasia shows the diverse ways in which nouns are affected: they are simply omitted or replaced by pronouns, by different near-homonyms, by figurative expressions, etc. Briefly, what is under attack are nouns as those morphological units which are least dependent on the context and, among such morphological units, not necessarily, but first and foremost, one observes a disappearance of grammatical subjects as the most independent constituents of the sentence which are the least conditioned by the context. Precisely such self-contained entities cause the greatest difficulties on this type of patient. Once in Paris Dr. Th. Alajouanine showed us a patient who had acquired a typical sensory aphasia as the result of an accident in the truck he drove. The greatest difficulty for him was to begin a sentence and, even more, a whole utterance with a nominal or pronominal subject. When we asked him, while he was writing, what he was doing, he answered, "J'écris". When we repeated the same question in referring to a student present, the answer was "Il écrit". But when I asked him, "What am I doing?", he had inhibitions before saying "Vous écrivez", and the same thing happened when a similar question was asked about a writing nurse. This curious difference is easily explainable: in French *vous* and *elle* are independent pronouns and act as grammatical subjects even in elliptic sentences ("Qui écrit!"—"Elle!"), whereas *je, tu, il*   are mere preverbs.

One agrees with the insistence upon the fact that the main loss in sensory aphasia afflicts not precisely subjects but nouns in general, because in contradistinction to agrammatism, which is primarily a syntactic disintegration, sensory aphasia, as a matter of fact, preserves syntax and affects primarily independent, indeed autosemantic morphological categories.

The relation between the treatment of nouns and verbs is one of the most cardinal questions for the study of language and language disturbances. The predominance of nouns over verbs in agrammatical patients has been demonstrated by J. Wepman (1973). A collaborator of Luria, L. S. Cvetkova, in her interesting Russian paper "Toward the Neuropsychological Analysis of the So-Called Dynamic Aphasia" (1968; *cf.* Luria & Cvetkova, 1968) showed how much more difficult the task of naming various verbs was for patients in comparison with their easier listing of concrete nouns. At the best two or three verbs were produced. May I tentatively confront these data with the new, still preliminary studies of R. W. Sperry and M. S. Gazzaniga on language comprehension in patients who have undergone split-brain operations (Gazzaniga, 1970). The comprehension of nouns flashed to the right hemisphere proved to be high with the exception of verbal nouns, whether unsuffixed *nomina actionis* or *nomina actoris* with the suffix *-er* (like "locker", "teller", etc.). Also, adjectives "were easily identified by the right hemisphere", with the exception of those derived from verbs, such as "shiny", "dried" and the like. With verbs "the performance level was poor". These data deserve to be compared with the relevant essay on the classification of language by the topologist René Thom (1973).

He posits a hierarchy of grammatical categories with the noun as the most stable and opposed in this respect to the verb, while verbal nouns are on the same level as verbs, and the adjective occupies an intermediate position between noun and verb. From the comparison of all these observations and insights it follows that the verb is a marked category, a superstructure in relation to the noun, and both the acquisition and disruption of language confirm this order. The confinement of "language comprehension in the right hemisphere" to pure nouns finds an explanation in their unmarked nature. The semantic mark of the verb, in contradistinction to the unmarkedness of the noun, is its reference to the time axis. Thus the immunity of the verb and of the syntactical sequence deployed in time are two natural and interconnected features of "temporal aphasias."

Many syntactic problems faced by the study of aphasia can be explained with reference to the hierarchy of linguistic structures, namely to the relation between the derived, marked, and the primary, unmarked variety. The examples often quoted from the speech of children or aphasics in languages which have different endings for the nominative and accusative cases are most instructive. Thus, in Russian, "*Papa* (nom.) *ljubit mamu* (acc.)" ("Dad loves mom") may be inverted without a change in the relation between the grammatical agent and the patient, which are signaled by two different inflectional suffixes, but aphasics and little children erroneously understand the inverted sentence, "*Mamu* (acc.) *ljubit papa* (nom.)", as "Mom loves dad", because the former word order is neutral, unmarked, whereas the latter is marked as expressive, and only the unmarked order is grasped by these listeners.   Dr. Goodglass' example, "the lion was killed by the tiger", tends to be interpreted by aphasics as "the lion killed the tiger", because in the usual, most normal word order the subject functions as an agent, whereas here it becomes the victim, and moreover, because the passive is a superstructure upon the active.

We cannot but agree with Dr. Goodglass in his rejection of the recent assumptions according to which aphasic losses effect only performance, but not competence (*cf.* Weigl & Bierwisch, 1973).   These surmises are built on a very narrowed and arbitrary conception of what competence is. Competence is far from being a static and uniform phenomenon.   Every speech community and each of its members dispose of a multiform competence, and our competence for speech production is quite different from that for speech perception; moreover, there is a substantial difference between competence in spoken and written language, again with a crucial subdivision into reading and writing. It would be an oversimplification to view these differences as mere varieties of performance.   The codes themselves differ.   Our competence for the explicit style of language is to be distinguished from our competence for different degrees of ellipsis. We must distinguish the verbal losses of an aphasic as speaker and as listener, and they can hardly be reduced by the scientific interpreter to questions of performance.   The changes in an aphasic's speech are not mere losses, but also replacements (*cf.* Jackson, 1958), and these replacements may be systematic, as for instance, the regularization of irregular verbs in the standard language, a phenomenon similar to the successive competences of a child in his approach to the mother tongue.   The peculiar forms of interrelation between the explicit and elliptic codes either in children or in aphasics are an intricate and imminent problem for the inquirer.

Although linguists have wide possibilities of describing and interpreting aphasic facts within the frame of language, without going beyond the linguistic level, let us recall that one of the great foreruners of aphasiology and, one may add, of modern linguistics, the neurologist John Hughlings Jackson, viewed aphasia as one of the possible semiotic disruptions which can occur either singly or concomitantly with other losses and preferred the term "asemasia" proposed by Allan McLane Hamilton as a generic name (Jackson, 1958; Hamilton, 1878). Of course, quite often the disruption can be limited solely to language, but we must consistently discuss the problems of language with regard to other problems of signs, such as gestures, graphics, music, etc., and their interrelations. Although we have significant research work on alexia and agraphia, studies of aphasia often neglect questions about the relation and difference between speech and script. When, for instance, aphasia is discussed only or primarily on the basis of the patient's oral reactions to written words, the problem of the significant difference between written and spoken words is not taken into account. There is also a noteworthy difference between how patients react in their utterances to objects and to pictures of objects, for pictures enter into the field of sings, they are semiotic facts. Such questions as the chasm between aphasia and amusia, clearly stated by E. Feuchtwanger in the early thirties (1932), could and should be connected with the amazingly frequent lack of ear and sense for music among the greatest poets extolled for the "musicality" of their verses, which here appears to be a mere metaphor.

Briefly, the further development of linguistic inquiry into aphasia demands a greater concentration on the description and classification of the purely verbal syndromes (*cf.* such recent studies as Pick, 1913), but with a constant attention to the whole semiotic framework. The progress of any linguistic study and of neurolinguistic research in particular depends on investigators taking more and more into account than the fact that the difference of patterns examined lies not only in the presence and absence of certain properties, but also—and even chiefly—in the difference between the predominant features, in short, in their different hierarchy.

References

Baudouin de Courtenay, Jan
    1885-86   "Z patologii i embryologii języka", *Prace filologiczne*, I.
Benveniste, Emile
    1966 *Problèmes de linguistique générale* (Paris).
    1966a "La form et les sens dans le langage" (Geneva).
Berko, J.
    1958 "The Child's Learning of English Morphology" *Word*, XIV.
Beyn, E. S.
    1957 "Osnovnye zakony struktury slova i grammatičeskogo stroenija reči pri afazijax", *Voprosy psixologii.*
Blumstein, Sheila E.
    1973 *A Phonological Investigation of Aphasic Speech* (The Hague: Mouton).
Cohen, D. & H. Hécaen
    1965 "Remarques neuro-linguistiques sur un cas d'agrammatisme", *Journal de psychologie normal et pathologique.*
Cvetkova, L. S.
    1968 "K nejropsixologičeskomu analizu tak nazyvaemoj dinamičeskoj afazii", *Psixologičeskie issledovanija* (Moscow University Press).
Dubois, J. & H. Hécaen et. al.
    1970 "Analyse linguistique d'énoncés d'aphasiques sensoriels", *Journal de psychologie normal et pathologique*, LXVII.

Feuchtwanger, E.
1932 "Das Musische in der Sprache und seine Pathologie", *Proceedings of the International Congress of Phonetic Sciences* (Amsterdam).

Gazzaniga, M. S.
1970 *The Bisected Brain* (New York: Appleton Century Grofts).

Gelb, A. & K. Goldstein
1924 "Über Farbennamenamnesie nebst Bemerkungen über das Wesen der amnestischen Aphasie überhaupt und die Beziehung zwischen Sprache und dem Verhalten zur Umwelt", *Psychologische Forschung*, VI.

Godel, R.
1957 *Les sources manuscrites du Cours de linguistique générale de F. de Saussure* (Geneva-Paris).

Goldstein, K.
1932 "Die pathologischen Tatsachen in ihrer Bedeutung für das Problem der Sprache", *Bericht über den XII Kongress der Deutschen Gesellschaft für Psychologie in Hamburg* (Jena).

Goodglass, H.
1968 "Studies on the Grammar of Aphasics", *Journal of Speech and Hearing Research*, XI.

Goodglass, H. & J. Berko
1968 "Agrammatism and Inflectional Morphology in English", *Journal of Speech and Hearing Research*, XI.

Goodglass, H. & J. Hunt
1958 "Grammatical Complexity and Aphasic Speech", *Word*, IV.

Goodglass, H. & S. E. Blumstein (eds.)
1973 *Psycholinguistics and Aphasia* (Baltimore: Johns Hopkins University Press).

Hamilton, Allan McLane
1878 *Nervous Diseases: Their Description and Treatment* (Philadelphia).

Hécaen, H. (ed.)
1972 *Neurolinguistique et neuropsychologie,* Langage, XXV.
Hécaen, H. & R. Angelergues
1965 *Pathologie du langage—l'aphasie* (Larousse).
Isserlin, M.
1922 "Über Agrammatismus", *Zeitschrift für die gesamte Neurologie und Psychiatrie,* LXXV.
Jackson, John Hughlings
1958 *Selected Writings,* II (New York).
Jakobson, Roman
1968 *Child Language, Aphasia, and Phonological Universals* (The Hague: Mouton). Translated from the German original published in 1941.
1971 *Studies on Child Language and Aphasia* (The Hague: Mouton).
1971a "Shifters, Verbal Categories, and the Russian Verb", *Selected Writings,* II (The Hague: Mouton).
Lecours, A. R. & F. Lhermitte
1973 "Phonemic Paraphasias", *Psycholinguistics and Aphasia,* ed. by H. Goodglass & S. E. Blumstein, (Baltimore: Johns Hopkins University Press).
Luria, A. R.
1964 "Factors and Forms of Aphasia", *Ciba Foundation Symposium: Disorders of Language* (London).
1966 *Higher Cortical Functions in Man* (New York: Basic Books). Translated from the Russian original published in 1962.
1973 "Basic Problems of Neurolinguistics", *Current Trends in Linguistics.*
1973a "Two Basic Kinds of Aphasic Disorders", *Linguistics,* CXV.
Luria, A. R. & L. S. Cvetkova
1968 "The Mechanism of 'Dynamic Aphasia' ", *Foundations of Language,* IV.

Pick, A.
1913 *Die agrammatischen Sprachstörungen* (Berlin).
1920 "Aphasie und Linguistik", *Germanisch-romanische Monatsschrift,* VIII.
Ross, A. S. C. et. al.
1964 "Edition of Text from a Dysphasic Patient", *Ciba Foundation Symposium: Disorders of Language* (London).
Salomon, E.
1914 "Motorische Aphasie mit Agrammatismus", *Monatsschrift für Psychologie,* I.
Tesnière, Lucien
1959 *Eléments de syntaxe structurale* (Paris).
Thom, René
1973 "Sur la typologie des langues naturelles: essai d'interprétation psycho-linguistique", *The Formal Analysis of Natural Languages,* ed. by M. Gross, M. Halle, M.-P. Schutzenberger (The Hague: Mouton).
Weigl, E. & M. Bierwisch
1973 "Neuropsychology and Linguistics", *Psycholinguistics and Aphasia,* ed. by H. Goodglass & S. E. Blumstein (Baltimore: Johns Hopkins University Press).
Wepman, J. M., et. al.
1973 "Psycholinguistic Study of Aphasia", *Psycholinguistics and Aphasia,* ed. by H. Goodglass & S. E. Blumstein (Baltimore: Johns Hopkins University Press).

*On the Linguistic Approach to the Problem of
Consciousness and the Unconscious**

In the second half of the 19th century the problem
of "the unconscious," as the author of a critical survey has
remarked, enjoyed a special popularity and was acknowledged as an important factor to be reckoned with when
treating diverse topics in the theory of behavior (Bassin,
55). Among the linguists of the time this issue was most
distinctly and most insistently raised by the young Baudouin
de Courtenay (1845-1929) and his brilliant disciple M.
Kruszewski (1851-1887). When still in the final stage of his
scholarly career, F. de Saussure (1857-1913), while discussing
a book published in 1908 by his student A. Sechehaye,
declared that Baudouin de Courtenay and Kruszewski "have
come closer than anyone else to a theoretical view of
language without going outside purely linguistic consider-
ations, yet they remain unknown to the majority of western
scholars" (IV, 43). The deplorable ignorance about the
theoretical positions of these two scholars has been repeatedly attested to by western linguists.

In Kruszewski's first scientific study, his Warsaw University thesis *Zagovory* (Spells)—a work written on a broad
ethnological theme (finished in January 1875 and published
the next year)—the established view of language as "a product of man's conscious activity" was opposed by the author's
own conviction that "human consciousness and will" exert
"only little influence" on the development of language.

Early in his Warsaw student years Kruszewski had

The Unconscious, III (Tbilisi, 1978).

attempted to peruse the text of Baudouin's first university lecture delivered in St. Petersburg in December 1870 and reproduced in *Žurnal Ministerstva Narodnogo Prosveščenija* in 1871 under the title, "Nekotorye obščie zamečanija o jazykovedenii i jazyke" (Some General Remarks on Linguistics and Language; see IT, I, 47-77). But on this first attempted acquaintance with Baudouin's text, the depth and breadth of its ideas proved beyond the novice's powers, as he himself acknowledged afterwards. However, five years later, while teaching school in the backwater town of Troick in Orenburg Province and amassing thereby the means for scholarly apprenticeship under Baudouin at the University of Kazan', Kruszewski once again, and this time with acute understanding, read that same lecture of 1870 and in a letter to Baudouin in September 1876 conferred his "inclination toward a philosophical, or rather, logical outlook on linguistics." The letter makes allusion to Baudouin's list of "forces acting in language": "I must say, I know nothing that could exercise in me a more magnetic attraction to the science of languages than the unconscious character of linguistic forces which prompted you, as I have only now noticed, to adjoin the term *unconscious* consistently in your enumeration of those forces. Happily for me, this fits perfectly with a notion that has long stuck in my mind,—I mean, the idea of the unconscious process in general, an idea that radically departs from the point of view of Hartmann. Precisely in order to clarify the difference, I spent my vacation engaged in laborious and tedious study of Hartmann's philosophy in its version by Kozlov. At the moment, of course, my pupils' lesson assignments have taken Hartmann's place but I hope to get back to him again" (the Polish original of this letter was published by Baudouin in *Szkice*, 134).

Already in Baudouin's master's thesis of 1870 (printed in Leipzig under the title "O drevnepol'skom jazyke do XIV-go stoletija" ([On Old Polish Before the 14th Century]

and defended by him at the Historical-Philological Faculty
of the University of St. Petersburg) among other major
points there is one that declares: " When considering even
the apparently simplest processes going on in language,
it is necessary to keep in mind the force of unconscious
generalization by the action of which a people subsumes
all the phenomena of its mental life under certain general
categories" (IT, I, 46).   Baudouin's inaugural lecture
in St. Petersburg, the one whose insistence on unconscious factors had so impressed Kruszewski, designates by
the term *forces* "general factors which bring about the
development of language and condition its structure and
content."   In the summary appended to this published
lecture the individual factors for the most part are marked
with a reference to their unconscious character (53). Among
such factors most prominently figure *"habit,* i.e. unconscious
memory" and on the other hand, "unconscious *oblivion*
and incomprehension (forgetting of what was not consciously
known and incomprehension of what could not be understood consciously); such forgetting and incomprehension
constituting not something inconsequential and negative
(as would be the case in conscious mental operations) but
something productive, positive and conducive to the new
by dint of its prompting unconscious generalization to move
in new directions."   This tendency to save the memory's
labor and to relieve it from an excess of mutually unbound
details Baudouin will later call (in his Derpt paper of 1888)
"a special kind of unconscious (*nieświadoma*) mnemonics"
(*Szkice,* 71).

By pointing to an analogy with biology, Kruszewski
enlarged upon his teacher's idea of disappearance as an
essential condition of development, and in his *Očerk nauki
o jazyke* (An Outline of the Science of Language) he held
consistently to the notion that "destructive factors" are
exceedingly beneficial for language" (chapters VII, VIII).
Some fifteen years later the issue of "oblivion" as a regular

base of linguistic transformations, the issue courageously
posed by Baudouin on the threshold of his scientific activities, was once again raised for discussion by   Arsène
Darmesteter (1846-1888) in the chapter "Oubli ou Cata-
chrèse" of his probing semantic book (1886).

In Baudouin's lecture of 1870 (IT, I, 38) "unconscious generalization" was characterized as *apperception,*
i.e. a force by the action of which people subsume all the
phenomena of their mental life under certain general
categories," and to this he added a comparison of the
systems of categories in language, which are   "joined
together by the force of unconscious generalization," with
"the systems of the celestial bodies which operate under
the influence of the force of gravity." If the connection
between a given linguistic entity and related formations
is "forgotten in the feeling of the people," it stands to the
side until it falls under the influence of "a new family of
words or category of forms." Baudouin insists that "people's
feeling for language is no fiction, no subjective illusion
but a real and positive category (function); it may be
defined in terms of its properties and effects, as it can be
verified objectively and proved by fact" (IT, I, 60). In
the interest of terminological accuracy, Baudouin and,
following him, Kruszewski preferred not to speak of "consciousness" of language but precisely of "a feeling for language," i.e. its unconscious, intuitive apprehension.

If "unconscious generalization, apperception," in
accordance with Baudouin's classification, "represents
the centripetal force in language," then, conversely, "unconscious *abstraction*, the unconscious tendency toward
division and differentiation," allows of comparison with the
"centrifugal force," and the "struggle of all the forces enu-
merated conditions the development of language."

Later, in Baudouin's "Obščij vzgljad na grammatiku"
([A General View of Grammar], a section of his *Podrobnaja
programma lekcij* [Annotated Program of Lectures] given

at the University of Kazan' during the academic year 1876-
77 (see IT, I, 102), their author returned to an examination
of all the forces acting in language which he had previously
identified, insisting anew on the unconscious character.
This time laws and forces were subjected to parallel examination as "*static,* i.e. operating in a synchronic position
(state) of language" and "dynamic, giving rise to the development of language." In connection with the question of
the influence of books "on the language of people with a
literary education," Baudouin, both in his Kazan' program
of 1876-77 (102) and in his lecture of 1870 (58f), was
prepared to acknowledge yet another of the forces acting
in language but this time a force "comparatively not very
powerful," namely "the influence on language of the human
consciousness": "Although the influence of the consciousness on language makes a fully conscious appearance only
among certain individuals, its effects are, nevertheless,
imparted to the whole people, and in that way the influence
of the consciousness can and does not impede the development of a language; it counteracts the influence of unconscious forces—forces which by and large promote a more
rapid development of language—and does so precisely for
the purpose of making language a common instrument
for the unification and mutual comprehension of all contemporary members of a nation, and its forebears and descen-
dants, as well. What results from this is a certain degree of
inertness in languages exposed to the influence of the human
consciousness in contradistinction to the rapid natural
movement of languages unaffected by that influence."

In Kruszewski's theory (1881*a*, 5; 1881*b*, 6) "language
is something that stands entirely by itself in nature" due to
the coparticipation of "unconscious-psychical phenomena"
(*unbewusstpsychischer Erscheinungen)* which are governed
by specific laws. The attempt to characterize the laws
underlying linguistic structure as well as its development was
one of the most original and, at the same time, most fertile

contributions made by the linguist during his all too brief career.

As for Baudouin, at the very start of the new century, he, in constrast to his own earlier insistent references to "unconscious factors," began attributing more and more significance to "the irrefutable fact of the intervention of consciousness into the life of language." In his words, "the tendency toward an ideal linguistic norm" is coupled with "the participation of the human consciousness in the life of language," in particular, "any linguistic compromise occurring between peoples speaking different languages" inevitably involves "a certain portion of conscious creativity" (from an article of 1908, "Vspomogatel'nyj meždunarodnyj jazyk" [An Auxilliary International Language] ; see IT, II, 152).

On the whole, Baudouin's view on the mental bases of linguistic phenomena evolved in the direction of bridging the gap between the conscious and the unconscious. At the end of his 1899 speech to the Copernicus Society of Cracow (see PF 1903, 170-171) he likened consciousness to a flame that casts light on single stages of mental activity; unconscious (*nieświadome*) psychical processes also have the capability of becoming conscious (*uświadomianie*) but their potential consciousness is actually identifiable with the unconsciousness (*nieświadomość*).

Statements on the subject in question made by Saussure during his tenure as professor in Geneva closely tally with the basic initial positions of Baudouin and Kruszewski. Saussure makes a clearcut distinction between the "unconscious activity" (*l'activité inconsciente*) of the participants in verbal communication and the "conscious operations" (*opérations conscientes*) of the linguist (II, 310). According to Saussure, "the terms a and b in and of themselves are incapable of reaching the sphere of conscious, while at the same time the very difference between a and b is always perceived by the consciousness" (II, 226). Drafts of his inaugural lecture in Geneva (the lecture was delivered in November of 1891) contain discussion concerning the participation in language phenomena of the act of will, in the course of which discussion Saussure revealed a series of gradations in both the conscious and the unconscious will (*dans la volonté consciente ou inconsciente*). With respect to all other comparable acts, the character of the verbal act seems to Saussure "the least deliberative, the least premeditated and at the same time the most impersonal of all" (*le moins réfléchi, le moins prémédité, en même temps que le plus impersonnel de tous*). Despite the considerable range of the differences he discussed, Saussure at the time acknowledged only the quantitative ones (*différence de dégres*) as real, relegating the qualitative differences (*différence essentielle*) simply to a deep-seated illusion (LV, 6).

Franz Boas (1858-1942), the founder of American anthropology and linguistics, devoted considerable attention to the topic of the unconscious factor in the life of language, principally within his extensive "Introduction" to Part I of the multi-volume series, *Handbook of American Indian Languages* (1911). A section in the second chapter of the "Introduction" is entitled "Unconsciousness of Phonetic Elements" and opens with the remark that "the single sound as such has no independent existence" and that it never enters into the consciousness of the speaker but exists only "as part of a sound complex which conveys a definite meaning." Phonetic elements "become conscious" only as a result of analysis. A comparison of words differing only in a single sound makes it clear that "the isolation of sounds is a result of a secondary analysis" (Boas, 23-24).

To the "Unconscious Character of Linguistic Phenomena" Boas returns in a substantial section (67-73) of the fourth chapter of that same "Introduction". This chapter is devoted to the relation between linguistics and ethnology, and it closes with a discussion of general linguistic topics from which the fifth, and final, chapter (78-43) turns directly to the "Characteristics of American Languages." Saussure's already mentioned thesis about "difference in degree of consciousness" between linguistic structure and parallel ethnological patterns is similar to Boas' thinking on "the relation of the unconscious character of linguistic phenomena to the more conscious ethnological phenomena." Boas believes that we are dealing here with a contrast that is "only apparent" and that "the very fact of the unconsciousness of linguistic processes helps us to gain a clearer understanding of the ethnological phenomena, a point the importance of which cannot be underrated. . . . It would seem that the essential difference between linguistic classifications never rise into consciousness, while in other ethnological phenomena, although the same unconscious origin prevails, these often rise into consciousness, and thus give rise to secondary reasoning and to re-interpretations" (67). Among phenomena which are experienced "entirely subconsciously" by the individual and by the whole people the author provides examples from the areas of beliefs, fashions, manners and the rules of modesty (67-70).

Boas saw the great advantage of linguistics in the always constantly unconscious character of the categories formed in language which makes it possible to investigate the processes underlying those categories without being misled by the "distorting factors of secondary explanations which . . . generally obscure the real history of the development of ideas entirely" (71).

Precisely the unconscious formation of grammatical categories and their interrelations, which act in language without their having to emerge into consciousness, prompts Boas to bring the available forces of linguistics to bear on an objective analysis of the systematic grouping of grammatical concepts characteristic for a given language or a given territorial league: "The occurence of the most fundamental grammatical categories in all languages must be considered as proof of the unity of the fundamental psychological processes" (71). At the same time, Boas warns investigators against repeated egocentric efforts to foist upon remote languages the system of one's own grammatical categories or the system of categories the scholar has become used to while working on languages close to his own (35 *ff*).

The problem of unconsciousness occupies a position of even greater importance in the work of Edward Sapir (1884-1939), the most prominent continuer of Boas' linguistic and anthropological vistas. In his frank review of the troubles faced by the science of language, "The Grammarian and his Language," Sapir advanced the thesis that the "psychological problem which most interests the linguist is the inner structure of language in terms of unconscious psychic processes" (SW, 152). If language possesses certain formal ways of expressing causal relations, the ability to receive and transmit them has nothing whatsoever to do with the ability to apprehend causality as such. Of these two abilities, the second bears a conscious, intellectual character and, like most conscious processes, requires a slower and more laborious development, whereas the former ability is unconscious and develops early without any intellectual efforts (155). In Sapir's judgement, the psychology that was available at the time his works were written did not seem altogether adequate to explain the formation and transmission of such submerged formal systems as are disclosed to us in the languages of the world. The language-learning process, "particularly the acquisition of a feeling for the formal set of the language," a process very largely unconscious, might possibly, "as psychological analysis becomes more refined," throw new light on the concept of "intuition," this intuition "being perhaps nothing more nor less than the 'feeling' for relations" (156).

In a work of the following year, "Sound Patterns in Language" (1925), in which he acutely posed the question of the speech sound systems, Sapir argued that an essential prerequisite for understanding phonetic processes is the recognition of a general patterning of speech sounds. An unconscious feeling for the relation between sounds in language promotes them to genuine elements of a self-contained "system of symbolically utilizable counters" (35). Further development in the study of the sound structure of language helped Sapir evolve a theory, in his 1933 article, "The Psychological Reality of Phonemes," regarding unconscious "phonological intuitions" and, in particular, to substantiate his own fruitful thesis, suggested by his years of fieldwork on the unwritten native languages of America and Africa, that not phonetic elements but phonemes are what the native member of the speech community hears (47 *ff*).

Of all Sapir's research works the one that most broadly covers the topic of the unconscious is the paper, "The Unconscious Patterning of Behavior in Society," which he prepared for the symposium "The Unconscious" held in Chicago during the spring of 1927. The author starts from the assumption that all human behavior, both individual and social, displays essentially the same types of mental functioning, both conscious and unconscious, and that the concepts of the social and the unconscious are by no means mutually exclusive (544). Sapir enquires why we are inclined to speak, "if only metaphorically," about forms of social behavior, of which the ordinary individual has no intelligible knowledge, as socially unconscious, and he answers his own question by pointing out that all those "relations between elements of experience which serve to give them their form and significance are more powerfully 'felt' or 'intuited' than consciously perceived" (548). "It may well be," Sapir goes on to say, "that, owing to the limitations of the conscious life, any attempt to subject even the higher forms of social behavior to purely conscious control must result in disaster." Most instructive in Sapir's eyes is the ability of the child to master the most complex linguistic structure, whereas "it takes an unusually analytical type of mind to define the mere elements of that incredibly subtle linguistic mechanism which is but a plaything of the child's unconscious" (549).

Unconscious patterning covers the entire range of features of speech, including, along with the directly significant forms, the inventory of sound units and configurations; and unconscious patterning belongs to the practice of the ordinary members of the speech community or in Sapir's phrase, "the unconscious and magnificently loyal adherents of thoroughly socialized phonetic patterns" (555). The paper's final conclusion is noteworthy. Sapir believes that "in the normal business of life it is useless and even mischievous for the individual to carry the conscious analysis of his cultural patterns around with him. That should be left to the student whose business it is to understand those patterns. A healthy unconsciousness of the forms of socialized behavior to which we are subject is as necessary to society as is the mind's ignorance, or better awareness, of the workings of the viscera to the health of the body" (558f).

In the final third of the last century and the first third of the present one, the topic of the conscious and unconscious as two co-participating factors in language became the object of wide-ranging discussion in the works of the leading theorists of linguistics, as is evident even from our brief review of statements by Baudouin, Kruszewski, Saussure, Boas, and Sapir. Their considerable value notwithstanding, it can hardly be doubted that their primary assumptions need careful and penetrating reexamination.

Only in recent time has linguistics taken cognizance of the "metalingual function" as one of the basic verbal functions. In other words, utterances can have direct reference to the linguistic code and its constituents. F. F. Fortunatov (1848-1914), in a remarkable lecture delivered to a congress of teachers of Russian in 1903, argued with good reason that "the phenomena of language, in a certain respect, themselves belong to the phenomena of thought" (II, 435). Metalingual operations constitute an important and indispensable part of our speech activity; through paraphrase, synonymy or via the explicit decoding of elliptical forms, they make it possible to assure full and accurate communication between speakers (see the present author's address of 1956 for the Linguistic Society of America, "Metalanguage as a Linguistic Problem" also included in this volume). Instead of unconsciously automatized means of expression, the metalingual function brings into play the cognizance of verbal components and their relations, thereby significantly reducing the applicability of the inveterate idea, repeated by Boas, that, supposedly, "the use of language is so automatic that the opportunity never arises for the fundamental notions to emerge into consciousness" and for these notions to come to be a subject of our thought (68).

In 1929 Aleksandr Gvozdev, a dedicated investigator of infant speech, provided an engaging answer to the crucial but long neglected question as to "how preschool children see the phenomena of language" (Gvozdev, 1961, 31-46); and this answer has brought in its train a rich, although still far from complete, series of evidential materials on the subject such, for instance, as we find in the works of Čukovskij, Švačkin, Kaper, and Ruth Weir. All these investigations and our own observations testify to a persistent "reflection about language on the part of children;" what is more, the child's initial language-acquisition is accompanied and secured by a parallel development of the metalingual function which enables the child to delimit the verbal signs he masters and to elucidate for himself their semantic applicability. "Virtually every new word stimulates an effort in the child to interpret its meaning," Gvozdev declares and, with that declaration in mind, cites questions and thoughts typical for children. For example: Are *sdoxla* and *okolela* the same?" (both verbs translate as "has died" with presumed reference to an animal and different emotional shades); "It's people you say *tolstyj* ('fat') about, but about a bridge you say *širokij* ('wide'); " "*Ubirajut* ('remove or dress up') means *ukrašajut* ('decorate'), doesn't it?"—asked in connection with the Christmas tree (40). Morphological analysis appears both in making up of words by children and in their conscious translation of a newly created lexical item into the habitual language: "The stove's all seived up (*prorešetela*)." Father "What?"—"It's gotten like a seive (*rešeto*)" (Gvozdev, 38).

Metalingual competence from the age of two turns the young child into a critic and corrector of the speech of surrounding people (Švačkin, 127) and even arouses in him not merely "unconscious" but also "deliberate antagonism" toward "adult" speech: "Mamma, let's agree you can call them [sled runners] your way *poloz'ja* and I'll call the my way *povoz'ja*. After all, they *vozjat* (from the verb *vozit'* "to carry by conveyance"), not *lozjat* (the child's ad hoc formation)" (Čukovskij, 62). Once they become aware of a pejorative tinge to the diminutive suffix *-ka*, the children whom Čukovskij observed, were ready to protest against extensive use of this morpheme: "It's not nice to say bad words. You should say *igola s nitoj* (child's ad hoc formation), not *igolka s nitkoj* ("needle and thread"). Or: "She's a *koša* (child's ad hoc formation instead of the usual *koška* "cat") because she's good. I'll call her *koška* only if she's bad." In the child's "conquest of grammar" his conscious awareness of linguistic categories generates creative experiments with such intricate morphological processes as aspectual opposition in verbs on the one hand— "*vyk, vyk i privyk* ("used, used and got used to"; *vyk* is the child's ad hoc formation of an imperfective past tense counterpart to the perfective past tense form *privyk*) (Čukovskij, 42); on the other hand, the child's effort to make a conscious connection between the form and the idea of grammatical gender may produce curious results: "*Luna* ("moon," feminine gender) is the wife of *mesjac* ("moon", masculine gender), while *mesjac* looks like a man"; "Is *stol* ("table," masculine gender) a daddy? *Tarelka* ("plate" feminine gender)—a mommy?" (Gvozdev, 44). A number of other typical examples of this same "linguistic consciousness" is given in Čukovskij's book (44): Why is he *papa* ("daddy")? He should be *pap*, not *papa* (*pap* is the child's arbitrary applications of masculine declension, "daddy", in view of the papa's chiefly feminine declension)"; "You, Tanya (a girl's name), will be the *sluga* (interpreted as a female noun because of its prevalently feminine declension) and Vov (a boy's name) will be a *slug* (transposed into a purely masculine paradigm)"; "You're a *muščin!*" (the child's ad hoc hyper-masculine version of *muščina*, "man", a masculine noun of chiefly feminine declension)"; "Maybe Musja (a girl's name) could have a *carapina* ("scratch", feminine noun), but I'm a boy—I'd have a *carap* (child's ad hoc masculine alteration of *carapina*)"; *Pšenica* ("wheat," feminine noun) is the mommy and *pšeno* ("millet grain," neuter noun) is her baby" [compare the coercion of grammatical gender and the possessive adjectives in the folk nursery rhyme—"For the woman's rye (*rož'*, "rye", is a feminine noun), For the man's oats (*oves*, "oats", is a masculine noun), For the girl's buckwheat (*greča,* "buckwheat", is a feminine noun), For the kiddy's millet (*proso*, "millet," is a neuter noun)— with the similar childlike interpretation of the neuter gender].

Underlying a piece of humorous play described by Gvozdev resides a conscious awareness of the bare syntactic matrix: Mother is sitting and knitting. Papa asks: "Who's that?" Two-year-old Ženja, according to Gvozdev, obviously intentionally: "Papa."—"Doing what?"—"Writing."—"Writing what?"—"Apple", and he was quite pleased with his answers (39). The minimal linguistic component follows suit, becoming the object of the child's conscious scrutiny: according to Gvozdev, a child, upon hearing the word *došlyj*("clever") in a conversation, made the remark: *"Došlyj*—that's easy to mix up with *doxlyj* ("dead"), as if "warning himself against confusing two words of similar sound, "differing only by a single distinctive feature.

There is evidence testifying to the conscious awareness on the part of small children to sounds and forms used by playmates who differ from them in age, in origin or who come from a different dialectical background. Finally, extremely instructive are references made by observers to the complex temporal aspect in the speech repertoire of young children. Such children not infrequently display an amazing ability to remember stages they are about to pass through or have already passed through in their own language experience. Children reveal an ambivalent attitude toward the new verbal material they have barely just acquired. They reveal either eagerness to use the new material as widely as possible or, on the contrary, mistrust and reluctance. For example, a little four-year-old girl, when asked by her father why she favored saying *vov*, although she had learned to pronounce the word correctly as *volk* ("wolf"), replied, "It isn't so awful and mean that way" (Gvozdev, 36).

The active role of the metalingual function remains in force, undergoing considerable changes, to be sure, throughout our entire life and maintains the constant flux between the conscious and the unconscious in all our speech activity. Incidentally, an analogy, productive in this connection, between ontogenetic and phylogenetic relations makes possible a comparison of the concatenated stages of child speech development with the dynamics of the language community, in which successive changes experienced by the community allow of conscious awareness on the part of the speakers and do so inasmuch as the start and finish of any change inevitably undergo a stage of more or less prolonged co-existence, which relegates separate stylistic roles to the initial and to the terminal points of development. If, for example, a linguistic change consists in the loss of a phonological distinction, the verbal code will temporarily maintain both the explicit start of the development and its elliptical finish, each serving as a stylistic variant in the over-all code and each, moreover, allowing for conscious aware-ness.

However, in our habitual use of language the deepest foundations of verbal structure remain inaccessible to the linguistic consciousness; the inner relations of the whole system of categories—indisputably function, but they func-tion without being brought to rational awareness by the participants in verbal communication, and only the inter-vention of experienced linguistic thought, equipped with a rigorous scientific methodology, is able to approach the innermost workings of linguistic structure consciously. Using a few graphic examples, we once demonstrated (see "Structures linguistiques subliminales en poésie," *Questions* of 1973, 280 *ff*) that the unconscious elaboration of the most hidden linguistic principles frequently constitutes the very essence of verbal art, however one gauges the dif-ferences between Schiller's belief that the poetic experience begins *"nur mit dem Bewusstlosen"* and Goethe's more radical thesis affirming the unconsciousness of all truly poetic creativity and casting doubt on the value of all author-ial rational excogitations.

The fact, observed by linguists, that the conscious and the unconscious factors form a constant bond in verbal experience needs the complementary interpretation of psychologists. We take the occasion of the Tbilisi Inter-national Symposium on the Unconscious to express the hope that the concept of "set" now in the process of development by the Georgian school of psychology will make it possible to define more closely the constant co-participation of the dual components in any kind of speech activity. As stated in the work of D. N. Uznadze (1886-

1950), the eminent initiator of research on "the experimental bases of the psychology of set," conscious processes do not exhaust the content of our mind; aside from such processes, something else takes place in a human being which cannot be said to occur in the consciousness and yet exerts a decisive influence on the entire content of mental life. Such is what has been termed *set*, and Uznadze was inclined to think that without its participation "no process as conscious phenomena could exist at all," and for the consciousness to start working in any particular direction, the presence of an active *set* is essential (179 *ff*).

A. S. Prangishvili, in his investigation of its governing principles, provided the concept of *set* with a new generalized definition: "Set invariably acts as an integral system with a constant group of characteristic features" (Prangishvili, 56)—a formulation distinctly closer to the linguistic diagnosis.

A. E. Sherozia, viewing conscious and unconscious experiences as colaterally subordinated and equally essential elements within "a single system of their relations," attaches to those experiences the "principle of complementarity" devised by Niels Bohr and insists on the necessity of a systematic confrontation of these two "correlative concepts" in view of the fact that "the concept of the unconscious is senseless taken independently of the concept of consciousness, and vice versa" (Sherozia, II, 8). Following through on Uznadze's thoughts about "a specific set for language," Sherozia points the way to a psychological explanation and dialectical resolution of linguistic antinomies such as "the duality of the nature of the word—its individuality and its generality." An assertion of Sherozia's in particular, that our word "always bears a greater amount of information than our consciousness is able to extract from it, since at the basis of our words lie our unconscious linguistic sets" (II, 446), corresponds with Sapir's supposition that to a large extent "the 'real world' is unconsciously built up on the verbal habits of the given group" and that not the same world "with different labels attached" but implicit differences of world outlook—"distinct worlds"—appear in the dissimilarity of languages (Sapir, 162). This same principle was broadened and made more incisive by Sapir's perspicacious disciple, B. L. Whorf, who directed his efforts to inquiring into the effect of dissimilarities in the grammatical structure of languages on the difference in the perception and appraisal of externally similar objects of observation.

Sherozia comes close, in turn, to Sapir's thoughts on the necessity for restricting conscious analysis in the everyday practice of language (see above) with his persuasive surmise: "If we were to require our consciousness to have at its command everything that occurs in our language and speech. . . it would have to reject such incessant labor" 'Sherozia II, 453).

The theory of the integral system of connections between conscious and unconscious mental experiences now being erected on the "principle of relation" (*princip svjazi*) promises new vistas and unlooked-for finds in the domain of language, provided, of course, that psychologists and linguists engage in genuine and consistent collaboration directed toward eliminating two impediments—terminological disparity and over-simplified schematicism.

References

Bassin, F. B.
 Problema bessoznatel'nogo (Moscow, 1968).
Baudouin de Courtenay, J.
 IT—Izbrannye trudy po obščemu jazykoznaniju, I-II (Moscow, 1963).
 "O psychicznych podstawach zjawisk językowych", *PF—Przegląd Filozoficzny,* IV (Warsaw, 1903), 153-171.
 Szkice językoznawcze, I (Warsaw, 1904).
Boas, F.
 "Introduction", *Handbook of American Indian Languages,* I (Washington DC, 1911).
Čukovskij, Kornej
 Ot dvux do pjati (Moscow, 1966, 19th edition).
Darmesteter, A.
 La vie des mots étudiée dans leurs significations (Paris, 1886).
Fortunatov, F. F.
 Izbrannye trudy, II (Moscow, 1957).
Gvozdev, A. N.
 Voprosy izučenija detskoj reči (Moscow, 1961).
Hartmann, E. von
 Filosofija bessoznatel'nogo, I-II (Moscow, 1873, 1875).
Jakobson, Roman
 "Metalanguage as a Linguistic Problem" (Ann Arbor, 1980). Included in this collection.
 Questions de poétique (Paris, 1973).
Kaper, W.
 Einige Erscheinungen der kindlichen Spracherwerbung im Lichte des vom Kinde gezeigten Interesses für Sprachliches (Groningen, 1959).

Kruszewski, M.
"K voprosu o gune" *Rus. Filol. Vestnik,* V (1881a).
Očerk nauki o jazyke (Kazan, 1883).
Ueber die Lautabwechslung (Kazan, 1881b)
"Zagovory kak vid russkoj narodnoj poèzii", *Izvestija Varšavskogo Universiteta* (1876).

Prangishvili, A. S.
Issledovanija po psixologii ustanovki (Tbilisi, 1967).

Sapir, E.
SW—Selected Writings (University of California Press, 1949).

Saussure, F. de
Cours de Linguistique générale, critical edition, ed. R. Engler, II (Wiesbaden, 1967); IV (Wiesbaden, 1974).

Sherozia, A. E.
K probleme soznanija i bessoznatel'nogo psixičeskogo, I-II (Tbilisi, 1969-1973).

Švačkin, N. X.
"Psixologičeskij analiz rannix suždenij rebenka. Voprosy psixologii reči i myšlenija", *Izvestija Akademii Pedagogičeskix Nauk,* VI (Moscow, 1954).

Uznadze, D. N.
Psixologičeskie issledovanija (Moscow, 1966).

Weir, Ruth Hirsch
Language in the Crib (Hague, 1962).

Whorf. B. L.
Language, Thought, and Reality (MIT Press, 1956).